Radical Promises
For Desperate Times

Key Publishing Company   *Port Huron, Michigan*

Radical Promises
For Desperate Times

How God Gets Us Through

by Pastor Bill Hossler

Key Publishing Company   *Port Huron, Michigan*

Key Publishing Company
3240 Pine Grove Avenue, Port Huron, Michigan 48060
810-984-5579   1-888-333-KEYS
FAX: 810-984-5595
E-Mail: keys@compucon-mi.com
Visit our Web Page: www:bwb.net/keys

Editing & Design by Justice Communications, 313 Huron Avenue,
Suite 202, Port Huron, Michigan 48060   810-982-3908

ISBN: 0-9650491-1-6

Contents

With Gratitude

I started this book ten years ago as a sermon series. I was so impressed with the promises—not the sermons—that I felt that I wanted to write about them. Surely others could profit from such a study, even as I had. Whether this book is for your devotional reading or for an in-depth study of a particular promise, I trust your love for and confidence in the promises of God grows as has mine.

The Author of the promises has guaranteed me so much that I felt compelled to acknowledge His greatness. I was telling Ron, my friend and parishioner how I felt and said, "I want to write this book in honor of Him." He suggested I make that the title of this book. His suggestion received a great deal of consideration. God is truly good and has promised us much.

I am indebted to my wife Margaret who has not tired of hearing me talk about this project for years and has constantly encouraged me to complete it. Without her inspiration, it would have died on the vine. Together we have seen God keep His promises. "Thanks Honey."

My friends Art, Terry and Ron have not only helped me dream about finishing this book, but have been inspirations and helpful critics. Our regular meetings to talk about book writing, discuss theology and plan for things in the future were challenging and enjoyable. I value their friendship and spiritual insights.

I asked for and received editorial help from several different sources. The careful attention each one provided was indeed helpful in moving the book closer to completion. Special thanks to Zaida Chidester, Ruth Carter, Jackie Weldy II, Dr. John Moran, Jack D'Arcy and Heather Marshall for reading the manuscript and providing helpful suggestions.

Thanks also goes to Jan, my secretary, for attention to details that keep me on course in the office, Colleen and Janice who were brought in on the project at the eleventh hour to help with title selection and to Gloria for her talents in graphic arts and a sense of what people are looking for.

I have had the wonderful privilege of pastoring the Newson Missionary Church and the Colonial Woods Missionary Church. Every pastor should be so blessed. My parishoners have taught me so much about God's faithfulness. In times of difficulty, sorrow, financial crisis or plenty, they have practiced what the Scriptures teach. Not only that, they have allowed me to share with them my journey of faith.

Last, but not least, I am indebted to my parents who have modeled what I have written. They provided a foundation that has been the bedrock of my spiritual life. My years in the ministry have made me clearly aware that many people are not nearly as fortunate as I am. Many could only dream about such a rich spiritual background. "Mom and Dad, your lives are gifts I highly treasure." (Mom died January 28, 1997.)

Pastor Bill Hossler

1

CHAPTER

Did God Mean Me?

"Let us hold unswervingly to the hope we profess,
for he who promised is faithful."
(Hebrews 10:23)

People are always looking for one of God's promises to fit some need or want in their lives. The classic example of this is the man who opened his Bible and ran his finger down the page until he felt "urged" to stop. When he looked at "his verse," he was startled to read "...and Judas went out and hanged himself." Disappointed, he tried again. This time his finger landed on the phrase "...go thou and do likewise." He edged his finger down the page one final time and stopped at the phrase "...and whatsoever you do, do quickly." These three phrases hardly gave him the direction or comfort he was looking for that day.

There are many teachings on just what the Christian life ought to be. Some recent teachings present the idea that Christians can have almost everything they want if they will only claim it. Other Christians contend that we can call on God for help, but God chooses to do for us only what He well pleases. Each group may talk about the promises of God, but approach the subject from a different point of view. This book is not a debate over who is right or wrong, but rather an exploration of specific promises and how they relate to the Christian.

The promises of God are the hope for the Christian. All Christians are dependent on God's promises for their very spiritual existence. Many of you would not wish to go on living without the promises from Scripture to sustain you and you hold on to them as dearly as a young child to a new toy. As you read through these chapters, you may be looking for a promise that relates to healing, forgiveness, or finances. Or you may be concerned about spiritual renewal or spiritual rewards. Whatever your need, the Word of God is full of His promises and hope for you.

Someone has calculated that the 31,173 verses in the Bible contain 30,000 promises—or approximately one promise for every verse (an exaggeration, I think). Dr. Everek Storms, the late editor of *Emphasis* magazine, stated that he had discovered a total of 8,810 promises with 7,487 of them directed from God to man, two from God to His Son, and 991 from one man to another. The New International Version of the Bible contains some version of the word "promise" over 200 times.

God is concerned about our welfare and comfort. He did not create us to leave us all alone to fend for ourselves. Jesus took great care to assure the disciples that He would leave them with special help when He went back to Heaven. He shows the same interest for you and me.

What Is A Promise?

Webster describes a promise as a "pledge to do or not do something specified; a cause or ground for hope, expectation, or assurance." I am immediately aware of the nature of a promise when I think back

"Whatever your need, the Word of God is full of His promises and hope for you."

to our children reminding me about promises I had made to take them sledding after work. If I started making excuses for why it was inconvenient to go right then, I soon heard, "But Dad, you *promised*." How does a Christian parent get out of that? If I didn't keep my word, how would my children believe what I said in the future or why should they believe what God says? My promise to take the boys sledding became my pledge to them and the foundation for their hope. They had probably gone around school telling their friends they were going sledding after school. If challenged, their response would have been, "My dad has promised!" That was all the assurance they needed.

A promise from God is His pledge of something He will do and the ground for our hope, expectation, and assurance. The assurance of your sins being forgiven is based on God's promise as seen in 1 John 1:9, "If we confess our sins, He... will forgive us our sins and purify us from all unrighteousness." Many times at an altar I have listened to a person read that verse and then asked: "If you confessed your sins, what has God done?" He or she would have to admit God's forgiveness, resting on the pledge that God would do what He promised.

Who Receives The Promises?

Not every promise is meant for every believer. I become concerned when I see people carelessly select a verse and "claim it" when it may not be for them at all. Some verses relate only to Israel or to some other group of people, while others are very specific about the timetable of their fulfillment. Other verses relate to the ungodly and the wayward. God has promised us something much better than fortune cookie promises. The sincere and diligent Christian can find scores of promises that apply to almost any situation of life.

Why Should I Believe A Promise?

Truth is at the very heart of a promise. There is little foundation for hope if the one making the promise cannot be trusted. I watch with interest the detailed discussions concerning treaties that are made between countries. I have to admit that I am skeptical when it comes to believing that all the promises in those treaties will be kept. Treaties are almost useless unless the promises are kept, even though such promises appear on paper.

When it comes to Biblical promises, it also is appropriate to ask "Why should I believe them?" Why should I get my hopes up? What is there about the promises I read in the Word of God that should give me confidence?

■ *God is always reliable.* One of the chief attributes of God is truth. He is absolute truth. There cannot be the slightest error or fabrication with God. When He speaks, things are absolutely as He says. Titus 1:2 says, "A faith and knowledge resting on the hope of eternal life, which God, who does not lie, promised before the beginning of time." Because it was impossible for God to go against His nature, Paul was confident that he had the promise of eternal life. Hebrews 6:18 again states that "It is impossible for God to lie." Therefore, because God could not promise us something He does not intend to fulfill, all of His promises are trustworthy.

■ *God is always faithful.* I have made promises I intended to keep, but they went unfulfilled because I either forgot or was careless in following through. This cannot happen with God. He can neither forget nor be careless. Paul reminds us of this attribute of God in 1 Thessalonians 5:24 when he says, "The one who calls you is faithful and He will do it." Hebrews 10:23 further confirms that "He who promised is faithful."

When I come across a promise such as "My God will meet all your needs according to his glorious riches in Christ Jesus"

(Philippians 4:19), I am assured God will fulfill that for me. God knows my every need. His very nature is one of truth and He would not have promised it to me if He did not mean it. Furthermore, God is faithful and will not get so busy doing other things that He forgets a promise.

■ *God is all powerful.* God's spoken Word was the only thing Moses trusted when he walked into Pharaoh's presence and announced a coming judgment or plague. Moses believed God had the power to do what He said.

It must have been frightening to approach the most powerful man on the earth and tell him the waters of the Nile River would be turned into blood unless the Israelites were set free (Exodus 7:17). I have often asked myself if I would have had the faith of Moses. I might have been tempted to try it out on a small pond before marching up to Pharaoh and making such a pronouncement.

"God has promised us something much better than fortune cookie promises."

When I get overwhelmed with problems and difficulties it helps me to think about the power of God. My spirit is renewed when I go over the details of some of the mighty miracles of Scripture and again remind myself there is no problem too great for God.

■ *God wants to help us.* When Moses wanted to know who was sending him to Egypt, God responded by giving His name as "the God who makes things happen." Other names of God are found throughout Scripture indicating God's concern for His people. Jehovah-Jireh refers to the "God who provides"; Jehovah-Shalom indicates "the Lord sends peace"; Jehovah-Rohi acknowledges that "the Lord is my Shepherd"; and Jehovah El Shaddai reminds us that "God is almighty." There are many other names given for God

> **"It was not enough for God to simply pass His promises on by word of mouth: He recorded them on written pages."**

which make for a very revealing and encouraging study.

We see God to be very interested in the day-by-day concerns of His children just by looking at His names. He is not an angry God waiting to strike us down, but rather He wants to provide us with everything we need to live Godly in this present world. I draw great strength from reviewing the various names of God and thinking about how each name can be applied to my life.

■   *The Bible is a reliable written record.* It was not enough for God to simply pass His promises on by word of mouth: He recorded them on written pages. We have them in black and white. Any time we choose, we can pick up the Bible and be reminded of His promises. Furthermore, we have the durability of the Word.

Down through the ages, monarchs, atheists and infidels have tried to destroy the Word of God. There have been those who boasted that their writings would make the Bible obsolete, but that has never happened—nor will it. Jesus gave us further hope when He said, "Heaven and earth will pass away, but my words will never pass away" (Matthew 24:35). Peter reinforces it by saying "The Word of the Lord stands forever" (1 Peter 1:25). The promises of God are ours as long as the Word of God endures.

Dear friend, it has been said, "Our future is as bright as the promises of God." If you are discouraged, weary, afraid or just wanting to discover more of God's great storehouse, look to the promises. In the promises, God has given you His pledge as an assurance and hope for your life both now and for eternity.

2
CHAPTER

Can I Be Sure?

*"For God so loved the world that he gave his
one and only Son, that whoever believes in him
shall not perish but have eternal life."*
(John 3:16)

A lady in our congregation asked me to visit her father
who was dying of cancer. He was aware of his condition
and was thinking about me conducting his funeral. I asked
her about his church and spiritual background so that I
could be more knowledgeable when I went to talk with him. She
shared that her father was a good man and very learned, but had no
church background and considered himself an agnostic.

I went to his hospital room one evening after visiting hours
were over, hoping to have some uninterrupted time to talk with

him. We exchanged friendly greetings and small talk, and then I ventured into the topic of his funeral service.

After covering some of the details of the service, I inquired about his spiritual condition and understanding. He did not demonstrate a grasp of what I was talking about, so I began to go through a presentation of the Roman Road plan of salvation, beginning with Romans 3:10 & 23 where we are reminded that all have sinned.

The concept of sin was a new idea to him. I wondered how this could be. How could one go through life and not comprehend this basic theological tenet? I prayed for wisdom. "Lord, here is a man who doesn't have many days to live and is unprepared to meet you. Besides that, here is his daughter and son-in-law who are new babes in Christ, and they are praying for his salvation. Please help me."

My mind was quickly drawn to the story of Nicodemus in John 3. I began to tell him the details of the passage and elaborated on what I understood to be its meaning. I explained about Nicodemus' credentials, that we obviously could not go back into our mother's womb, that we are changed by the power of the Holy Spirit, and that because God loves us He sent Jesus to give us eternal life. I explained it to him in great detail.

After I finished sharing with him and answering his questions, I felt I had not gotten through at all. It seemed he was somewhat bored with the subject. Having gone as far as I could, I concluded our conversation for the evening and had prayer with him.

A couple of days later I returned to the hospital to visit him again. As I walked into the room there was a nurse doing considerable work with him. I prayed quietly, asking God to clear the room so I could have uninterrupted time to again pursue spiritual issues with this terminally ill man. The nurse left after several minutes and we were not interrupted at all during the rest of my visit. I had not been there too long when he said, "Can we talk again about what we were discussing the other evening?" I thought he meant about the service so I said, "About the funeral service?"

> "What a privilege to be able to offer John the promise of being restored to a right relationship with God."

"No," he said, "About that man you were telling me about that went to Jesus at night."

"You mean Nicodemus?"

"Yes, that's the man" was his reply. I was very surprised by his interest, because I had come to the hospital thinking I would have to push the subject of salvation.

It was with joy that once more I reviewed the subject of being born again—how necessary it is and how I understand it happens. After talking about it for some time, I said, "John, would you like to receive Christ into your heart and be born again?" Without a moment's hesitation, he said, "Yes." I prayed the following prayer and asked him to repeat it after me: "Dear Jesus, I thank you for dying on the cross for me. I ask you to forgive my sins and come into my life. I want to be born again. Thank you for doing it. In Jesus' Name, Amen." He sincerely prayed that simple prayer and that morning became a child of God.

A week or so later I visited him in his home. His wife, most of the children and a number of the grandchildren were in the house when I visited. When it came time for me to lead in Scripture reading and prayer, he stopped me and said so his family could hear, "Pastor, I want all of my family to come to this belief." What a thrill that was for me. This confirmed to me that the Holy Spirit had opened his heart and helped him to understand spiritual truths at the eleventh hour of his life.

He passed away about a week after that last meeting. Since then, his wife and several of his grandchildren have accepted Christ into their lives.

What a privilege to be able to offer John the promise of being restored to a right relationship with God. This is God's design for each of us, despite Adam and Eve's disastrous fall in the Garden.

The Great Need For Rebirth

The early verses of John 3 record for us the story of Nicodemus. In some ways, Nicodemus is a representative of all the human race. Many would agree that he is a very good choice. He was a leader and had so many of the qualities that one is looking for:

■ *He was a religious man—a Pharisee.* The Pharisees were a select brotherhood with as many as 6,000 members at one time. As a religious sect they tried to keep the law to the fullest extent possible while another group of religious leaders, the Scribes, concentrated on explaining and interpreting the Scriptures.

■ *He was a well educated man.* The fact that he was a Pharisee reveals he had a much higher than normal education. Besides that, his Greek name indicated the desire, on the part of his parents, to incorporate into his life all the best of the Greek culture.

■ *He was a great community leader.* This man was not a "down and outer." He was part of the top echelon of society. He was a member of the Sanhedrin which was the Executive, Legislative, and Judicial branches all wrapped up in one. This body governed almost all of Jewish life.

But, despite all of his good qualities, there was one problem that Jesus recognized and addressed immediately.

Nicodemus Was Spiritually Deficient

You may ask, "Why do you say that?" Well, take note of a couple of clues. In verse 2, Nicodemus wants to flatter Jesus and also be polite so he acknowledges that God obviously empowered Jesus as evidenced by the miracles He performed. Jesus very abruptly changed the subject in verse 3. It appeared that Jesus didn't even hear what Nicodemus had said. Jesus quickly replies with, "You

> "We are born
> physically
> alive, but
> spiritually
> dead."

must be born again." It seemed as though Jesus was saying, "Nicodemus, I am going to cut through all the formalities and get to the heart of the matter. You don't really know what's important. There are spiritual things you don't understand."

Nicodemus' deficiency is pointed out by Jesus again in verse 9. Nicodemus asked another question about the new birth. Jesus responds by saying, "You call yourself a teacher and you do not understand these things?" Now remember, Nicodemus was religious, a quality man and a community leader, but these attributes were not sufficient. He needed to be able to discern the things of the Spirit to live pleasing to God.

Spiritually speaking man was given a spirit so he could receive messages from the Divine Brain (God Himself) concerning spiritual matters. In the garden Adam and Eve were told that if they ate from the tree of "knowledge of good and evil," they would surely die (Genesis 2:17). They died spiritually immediately upon eating the fruit. The nerve connecting the Brain and the muscle was severed.

This condition, known to doctors today as Myasthenia Gravis, is described by James Montgomery Boice in his expositional commentary on *The Gospel of John*:

> "...In the human body the brain normally originates the signal for a muscle to expand or contract. The signal is sent to the muscle through a nerve and is received in the muscle by an apparatus known as the motor-end-plate. [With Myasthenia Gravis,] the motor-end-plates are missing. Consequently, the signal is sent to the muscle through the nerves, but it is never received by the muscle... does not respond... and eventually withers away and dies."

In a sense, when Adam and Eve sinned, the motor-end-plate no longer could receive the message of God. The Apostle Paul writing in Romans 5:12 says that sin passed upon all men and because of that sin all died. Paul further states that we are all dead in trespasses and sins. Nicodemus was not receiving the spiritual truth he needed to be receiving. Remember, if he is a representative of the human race and he received his problem from Adam, then we are all deficient. There is an absolute need for a rebirth for all of us.

"I tell you the truth" is an interesting little phrase found in verses 3, 5 and 11. Jesus seemed to be saying, "Nicodemus, I want you to understand this without any doubt. This is *the* truth. I don't care what you've learned in books—this is *the* truth."

In verses 3, 5 and 7, Jesus used the words "unless" and "must" when talking about the necessity of the new birth. A rebirth is not an optional thing. **YOU MUST BE BORN AGAIN**, if you want to see the Kingdom of God and if you want to know what life with God is like for all eternity. **Unless a man is born again he cannot see or inherit the Kingdom of God.**

The Manner Of Our Rebirth

Through the years, "born again" has taken on a variety of meanings. If a politician changes his stance on a particular issue the headlines may well say, "He's born again." If a person makes some changes and turns over a "new leaf," many say he's "born again." If a movie star makes some kind of shallow spiritual commitment, the magazines describe the experience as being "born again." Is that what really happens?

The concept of being born again has nothing to do with revising convictions, turning over new leaves, or revitalizing careers. It's what God does in us. That's what makes the difference. A politician who turns over a new leaf or changes his policies does it, not God. He's not born again from God in the spiritual sense.

If the Scriptures are true—and they are—then when Adam and Eve died spiritually in the garden of Eden, the sentence of death was also passed to all of us.

> **"The first step in our restoration is the admission of our own guilt and the need for God's intervention."**

We are born physically alive, but spiritually dead. Therefore we need to be reborn in our spirit so that we can again have the relationship Adam and Eve had with God in the beginning. We need to be restored to that original position by God. Jesus said, "Nicodemus—unless you are born again you will not see or inherit the Kingdom of God." You can't get in without being born again. It can't happen.

In John 3:5, Jesus answered, "I tell you the truth, no one can enter the kingdom of God unless he is born of water and the Spirit." Jesus made it very clear in John 1:13 that this new birth is from God when He said, "Children born not of natural descent, nor of human decision or a husband's will, but born of God."

If God doesn't do it, then we are not born again. It's a spiritual thing. Unless God does it, it doesn't matter what we say or how we may attempt to change, it isn't real. **Being born again is a miraculous event that is an act of God.**

Nicodemus asked how being born again can happen? "Can I go back a second time into my mother's womb?" Jesus said, "No, it's like the wind: you can't see where it comes from or where it goes, but you know it happens. This is the way it is of everyone born of the Spirit." While we cannot bring about our new birth, we can start the process that enables God to do it in us.

The first step in our restoration is the admission of our own guilt and the need for God's intervention.

A former governor of Texas once spoke at a prison. After addressing a large group, he volunteered to meet with some inmates privately. A number of them came to him complaining that they had gotten a bad rap; that they had been falsely accused or had been charged incorrectly. Finally one man came to him and said, "Gov. Neff, I did exactly what I was charged with and I deserve to be here. I have served quite a long time. If you would see your way to grant me a pardon, I will seek to live a life that would show that you made the right the decision." Governor Neff pardoned him.

Admitting our sins and asking for Christ's pardon is what we need to do.

Rebirth
Produces A Difference

Starting in verse 11 Jesus changes from the personal pronoun "I say unto you" and "I tell you the truth" to the plural pronoun "we." He uses it in phrases such as "**we** speak of what **we** know and **we** testify to what **we** have seen but still you do not accept **our** testimony." He is not saying, "Nicodemus, you have not accepted **my** testimony" but "you have not accepted **OUR** testimony." What was Jesus talking about?

There are several interpretations as to what Jesus meant here. I think Jesus is saying, "You have seen the changed lives of many individuals such as Mary Magdalene and still you will not accept the validity of what has happened." You will not accept the difference that God can make in a person's life.

Dr. Harry Ironside was on a street corner in San Francisco where the Salvation Army was holding a street meeting. The captain recognized Dr. Ironside and asked him to step to the front of the group and give a testimony.

He did so, telling how his life was changed by someone preaching the message of the cross and the resurrection. As he continued there was a man on the outside of the crowd listening intently. When Dr. Ironside finished the man took a card out of his pocket and wrote something on the back and gave it to him. Dr. Ironside looked at the card and recognized the name immediately. The man was a well known agnostic.

The note on the back of the card said, "Sir, I challenge you to debate with me the question, 'Agnosticism verses Christianity' in the Academy of Science Hall next Sunday afternoon at four o'clock. I will pay all the expenses."

Dr. Ironside looked again at the card and read it to the crowd. Then he said, "I will be glad to debate the gentleman but only under two conditions: one, I ask this gentleman to bring first of all a man who has known the depths of sin, a man whose life has been scarred and ruined by the things in which he has been involved.

Furthermore, that such a man has been inspired by agnosticism and has gone out and changed his life, has been restored to his family and has developed a purpose for living.

Two, that he find a woman who also knew what it was to live in the depths of sin and whose life had been scarred and ruined by the way she had lived, yet a woman whose life was dramatically changed for the good by the virtues of agnosticism.

"Now if this gentleman will do that, I will bring 100 men and women whose lives have been gloriously and wonderfully changed by the preaching of the gospel: people who have been taken out of the gutter and transformed and renewed in their spirit."

"Christianity changes people..."

Dr. Ironside turned to the Captain of the Salvation Army Corp and said, "Do you think you have any people you could send along with me?" Without a moment's hesitation the captain said, "I'm sure we can have forty from our corps alone."

Dr. Ironside said to the rest of the crowd and the man standing there, "I don't think I'll have any trouble getting the other sixty converted individuals from the other Army Corps and churches in town. The man raised his hand and said, "No deal" and walked away. Why? Christianity changes people and agnosticism does not.

Jesus spoke pointedly to Nicodemus because he had not believed the witnesses. In essence Jesus was saying, "You have seen the changed lives of all these people but you do not accept it."

Jesus—The Promise Of Our Rebirth

"Just as Moses lifted up the snake in the desert, so the Son of Man must be lifted up, that everyone who believes in him may have eternal life." (John 3:14-15)

The Old Testament provides shadows of what was to come in the New Testament. **Photographs snapped in the Old Testament are fully developed in the New Testament.** Such a picture is given in Numbers 21.

When the Children of Israel were in the wilderness of Sinai, they began to complain about the leadership of Moses. The cafeteria's selection of food was just not right. The stores were not stocked with enough clothes. They began to complain and ask why they had not remained in Egypt.

God sent venomous snakes into the camp in response to their complaining. Shortly after the people were bitten by the snakes, they died. The people begged Moses to help them. God told Moses to "make a snake of bronze and put it up on a pole; anyone who is bitten can look at it and live." (Numbers 21:8)

> "Eternal life belongs to all who believe in Jesus and receive Him into their heart."

They were not sent to the shopping mall for clothing or supplies nor to the hospital for some medical cure. Neither were they able to find healing by means of some path of self reformation. They needed to be healed and reformed. They needed to clean

> **"No one can gain salvation or be born again by their own efforts... Salvation comes only by looking to the Christ who died on the cross."**

up their act and attitude, but they weren't able to do so by themselves. They weren't even told to band together and fight the serpents like some wild adventure movie where only two people are left who can save the planet. Neither were they told to pray to the serpent on the pole or buy some relics of the pole. They weren't told to do any of these things.

The bitten Israelites were simply instructed to turn and look at the serpent to be healed. They couldn't work for their healing. There was no anti-snake venom. Neither were they able to concoct any other "home remedies" for curing their illness.

The Children of Israel kept the serpent as a reminder of their miraculous healing. However, years later some of the people began to burn incense to the serpent. Hezekiah the king recognized that this was wrong and destroyed the pole (2 Kings 18:4).

In the Middle Ages there were some enterprising people from the Middle East who were selling "pieces of the cross." People seemed to feel that possessing what they thought was this special piece of wood would bring them good luck. What many of them failed to realize was that enough pieces of the cross were sold to build several huge cathedrals. The whole scheme was a sham.

Some people today believe that wearing a cross around their neck or placing a statue in their home will bring good luck and make them more fit for heaven. These things may be nice reminders, but they do nothing to prepare our spirit to meet God. These devices do no more for us than the actions of the Children of Israel after they had been bitten by the snakes.

Jesus gave the clear meaning of this event when he said in John 3:14-15, "Just as Moses lifted up the snake in the desert, so the Son of Man must be lifted up, that everyone who believes in him may have eternal life."

Friends, no one can gain salvation or be born again by their own efforts. We cannot be restored by ourselves. **Salvation comes only by looking to the Christ who died on the cross.** Jesus said in John 3:16, "For God so loved the world that he gave his one and only Son, that whoever believes in him shall not perish but have eternal life."

John 3:16 is one of the greatest verses ever penned. Karl Barth, the famed theologian, was in the United States lecturing at several universities when a young man asked him, "Dr. Barth, what is the greatest thought that has ever gone through your mind?" He thought for a moment and said, "Jesus loves me this I know for the Bible tells me so. That's the greatest thought I have ever had."

Besides John 3:16 being the greatest verse, someone has suggested it also contains the greatest gift, the greatest invitation and the greatest promise.

Notice the promise: "whoever believes in him (Jesus) shall not perish but have eternal life." (John 3:16) What a promise!

Yes... You Can Be Sure

I was standing in the foyer of my first church on the last night I would pastor that congregation. My wife and I were moving to another city during the coming week.

We were talking with a young couple that we had been privileged to lead to the Lord several years earlier. As they were leaving that evening, I remember the wife saying to us, "Since we have come to Christ we all have the promise of seeing each other in heaven one of these days. Our lives have been changed for all eternity." Wow! That statement had a great impact on me. It put a renewed meaning into my work.

"It doesn't matter where you are spiritually right now, to what depths of sin you may have gone, how lacking your spiritual heritage is or anything else you think may disqualify you. None of your past leaves you outside of God's reach."

God has given us the wonderful promise in written form that when we look to Christ for salvation and accept His gift, He includes our name in the Lamb's book of life.

I don't know how many years there will be between my death and that of the man I talked about in the opening of this chapter. But I am confident that if scores of years separate us, we will still see one another again. **Eternal life belongs to all who believe in Jesus and receive Him into their heart.**

It doesn't matter where you are spiritually right now, to what depths of sin you may have gone, how lacking your spiritual heritage is or anything else you think may disqualify you. None of your past leaves you outside of God's reach. For "whoever believes in Jesus shall not perish but have eternal life" (John 3:15).

But how does one experience this promise? How does our rebirth come about? What does it mean to believe? Is it sufficient simply to agree that Jesus is the Son of God? Is that enough?

J.G. Patton, pioneer missionary to New Hebrides Islands, went to the natives and discovered they had no written language so he put their language into written form. He was looking for a word for "faith", but could not find one. The natives didn't seem to have any word in their vocabulary that compared. One day he went with a native hunting in the mountains. After they had killed a deer, they tied its feet together, put a pole between its legs and started down the mountain. They were tired and exhausted by the time they reached the compound. They laid the deer down and dropped into their chairs. The native said, "My, its good to stretch yourself out here." Patton jumped up and went to his study and wrote, "Faith— to stretch oneself out and rest."

When asked what he had to do to be saved, Paul could have said to the Philippian jailer, "stretch yourself out and rest on the Lord Jesus Christ and you shall be saved" (Acts 16:31).

We could rewrite John 3:15 to say, "that everyone who "stretches himself out on the Lord Jesus Christ and rests" may have eternal life" or John 3:16 could be revised to say, "For God so loved the world... that whosoever stretches himself out and rests on the Lord Jesus Christ shall be saved." That's what it means to believe.

Have you stretched out on Christ and rested? Are you tired and finished with trying to reform yourself? You only have to look to Him to be saved.

You only have to stretch yourself out on Him and rest on His finished work on Calvary and you will be saved. Why not claim this wonderful promise of rebirth today?

3

CHAPTER

What Is God's Will?

"A man's steps are directed by the Lord"
(Proverbs 20:24)

Prior to my graduation from high school, I worked on a farm to earn money for spending and college. One particular day, while I was cultivating corn, I was deeply engrossed in thinking about what I should do with my life. I knew God had called me into full-time Christian service and I would spend my life spreading the gospel, but I wasn't sure where or how. I was perplexed over whether I should get into missionary aviation or go into some other type of ministry. Even though I was enamored with the thought of flying, I was content to do whatever God wanted me to do. How would I know? My choice of colleges would be affected by the decision I made. What should I do?

I pondered and prayed over this decision. My mind was far from the tender corn stalks I was cultivating. "Lord, why don't you answer? This is very important to a 17-year-old kid who wants to be in the center of Your will. How am I to know Your will if You won't answer me?" After spending most of the morning deep in thought, I remember walking to the house for the noon meal when a Bible verse suddenly came to me. I'm sure I must have learned it in church, but I did not know where it was located.

That day became a day I have never forgotten. When counseling scores of people since then, I think back to that day and with confidence talk to them about seeking the Lord's direction for their life. God gave me a promise that day that became personal for me. I was certain that I would not be left in the dark about the future, but in God's time He would give direction to my life. That promise is found in Proverbs 3:5 and 6, "Trust in the Lord with all thine heart; and lean not unto thine own understanding. In all thy ways acknowledge him, and he shall direct thy path." (KJV)

Although I certainly wasn't the first person to discover those verses, they became real to me that day. The load of concern lifted from me. I believed that simple promise was true. I fully expected God to direct my path. He had to. He had promised that He would, if I put Him first in my life and wanted His will for my life.

When we think of God's promises that relate to finding His will for our lives, there are two basic areas we want to consider, **Specific Direction and General Direction.**

Specific Direction

Specific Direction relates to matters such as "Should I look for another job?"... "What should I do with my life?"... "What college should I attend?"... "Does God want me to buy this new car?"... "Should I marry Margaret?"... "Does the military service or college fit into God's plan for me?"... and many other specific actions in one's life.

While these decisions may trouble our thoughts the most, they do not occupy as much time as we might think. At best, these

> "Once our general and basic directions are in line with God's will for our life, He gives us perimeters in which to operate."

decisions are made in a matter of hours, days or months. Most of them do not take years to decide even though we may spend time in prayer, fasting and other means to seek the will of God.

General Direction

Things concerned with general or basic direction do not seem nearly as urgent, but are far more important, more far reaching and much more influential. The general things are where we really live: the foundation used to determine the specific details of life. The general basics are such things as my salvation, my purpose in life, my priorities, and my principles.

For example, if God is the number one priority in my life, many things with which I might otherwise struggle will automatically fall away or will be understood in a clearer light. Or if my life is governed by some well established principles much decision making is already cared for. I will not have as much difficulty in discovering God's will for my life.

My wife Margaret and I were once talking to a young woman who professed faith in Christ. She was a young mother with several small children. She said she had been praying about whether she should go to this other city to be a dancer in a night club. She decided it was OK. We disagreed with her. To us, there was no need to pray. That was a decision she should have had no trouble in making except that her priorities and principles were not in order. Her divine direction was missing. She prayed about some specifics when she first needed to settle on the general areas. The specifics would have taken care of themselves. If she had considered how her influence would be hindered, the type of company she would be keeping, how she would be putting herself in the way of temptation and other clear teachings from Scripture, she wouldn't have even considered going. Her general understanding of the ways of God would have given clear direction in the specifics.

Therefore, it is the general areas of life that need more of our attention than do the specifics. In fact, **once our general and basic directions are in line with God's will for our life, He gives us perimeters in which to operate.** It is something like playing the game of football within the boundary lines. As long as we stay in bounds, the decisions are ours to make. I am not convinced that God is too concerned whether you buy a blue or a red dress, or a car with two or four doors. Rather, if your basic priorities are in line, you have what is necessary to make most decisions.

For those areas where we don't feel comfortable making them by ourselves, there are also some brief guidelines for us to follow.

F. B. Meyer was with the captain of a ship that was coming into the harbor. Mr. Meyer asked the captain how he could find the entrance to the harbor and stay in the channel when it was so dark. The captain pointed to two different lights off in the distance. He said, "when the two lights line up to form just one light then I know I am right on course". Likewise, there are basic rules that need to line up for us to know God's will.

1. What does God's Word say? Is what I desire in keeping with the teachings of Scripture? God will never direct you contrary to His Word. The Bible does not give us a definitive word on every decision we will make. Therefore, if our decision does not violate the Word in letter or in spirit we have passed the first test.

2. What do the circumstances suggest? Let's say you are in the market for a different car. You've always dreamed of owning a Cadillac but your budget is going to be stretched by a beat up Chevy. The circumstances would suggest that the Cadillac is likely not God's will for you. That is not to say that some day that would not become a reality, but for now that is not God's choice.

"Just because circumstances would allow you to do a certain thing does not mean that God wants you to do it."

On the other hand, we are not necessarily to walk through every open door. Just because circumstances would allow you to do a certain thing does not mean that God wants you to do it. You may very well be able to own a Cadillac or even several Cadillacs, but that may not be the best test for knowing God's will. The apostle Paul says, "Everything is permissible for me—but not everything is beneficial. Everything is permissible for me—but I will not be mastered by anything" (1 Corinthians 6:12).

Over the years I have observed pastors move from one church to another and wondered if it is God's will that the average pastor change every 3.5 years? It seems that too often we hit a crisis in our current charge and at about the same time we are contacted by another church and assume the two events go together. We think the circumstances merit the move. It may not be so. Point #2 primarily reminds us that God works in an ordered pattern for our lives.

3. *What is my inner sense of direction?* What does the Holy Spirit seem to be saying to me at this particular time and in this situation? We need to learn to discern the still small voice of the Spirit.

Staying On Course
The road that God has mapped out for us has many billboards and road signs that dot the landscape. They are of a diverse background with some signs placed there by the enemy of our souls and others by our Creator and Keeper. God has placed many and varied promises along the path of life. I want to help you see a few that will keep you on course.

■ *God will never lead you contrary to His revealed will.* The Bible is the final authority in all matters of faith and practice.

Periodically someone will say that God told them to do something that is contrary to Scripture. The feeling seems to be that God sets aside His eternal standards for one individual. But such is not the case. **Scripture and the inner witness will always agree when we are in God's will.** The following verses are just a few reminders that God's Word or ways do not change like the seasons.

"But you remain the same, and
your years will never end."
(Psalms 102:27)

"I the Lord do not change."
(Malachi 3:6)

"....you remain the same, and your
years will never change."
(Hebrews 1:12)

"Jesus Christ is the same yesterday
and today and forever."
(Hebrews 13:8)

"The Father of the heavenly lights,
who does not change like
shifting shadows."
(James 1:17)

■ *Wherever He leads us He will go with us.* I sat in a small home in China listening to a husband tell about his years in a Communist prison because of his Christian faith. The husband had spent nearly 23 years in prison and his wife 19 years. The word of exhortation from this gentleman to us was taken from Revelation 2:10 which says, "Do not be afraid of what you are about to suffer... Be faithful even to the point of death, and I will give you the crown of life."

"Scripture and the inner witness will always agree when we are in God's will."

We then turned to his wife, who up to this point had been rather quiet, and asked, "What helped to hold you faithful during all those years of imprisonment?" With a smile on her face that will be forever etched in my mind, she started to sing an old hymn of the church. It didn't take us long to catch on to the hymn or understand something of the faith of this spiritual giant. With that beautiful smile and from the depths of her heart she began to sing, "All the way my Savior leads me, what have I to ask beside? Can I doubt His tender mercy who through life has been my guide? Heavenly peace divinest comfort, ere by faith in Him to dwell, for I know what ere befall me, Jesus doeth all things well."

By the time she had finished singing, tears were streaming down my face as I realized I had just received a valuable lesson about the presence of God. I had heard first hand what I had only read about in books. Here was a dear saint of God who had gone through the "fire" of tribulation telling us that God was with her.

The promise for God's children is that He will never leave us or forsake us. Therefore, whether your road leads to pleasant places or through the shadows and darkness of a prison camp, God is always there.

The Psalmist knew it when he said, "Even though I walk through the valley of the shadow of death, I will fear no evil, for you are with me" (Psalms 23:1). Paul spoke of it when he said that "The one who calls you is faithful, and he will do it" (1 Thessalonians 5:24).

One verse that speaks of this truth in principle, if not in specifics, is Psalms 23:1 which says "The Lord is my shepherd." Since the shepherd is always leading the flock, we know that God is always going ahead of us and through our trial with us.

David Livingston had spent sixteen years in Africa, but had not faced such risk and peril. He was surrounded by hostile, angry natives in the heart of Africa. He was fearful for his life and considered fleeing during the night. But, something happened that changed his mind and gave him peace in his hazardous situation. He recorded it in his diary for January 14, 1856:

'Felt much turmoil of spirit in prospect of having all my plans for the welfare of this great region and this teeming population knocked on the head by savages tomorrow. But I read that Jesus said, "All power is given unto Me in Heaven and in earth. Go ye therefore, and teach all nations, and lo, I am with you always, even unto the end of the earth." It is the word of a gentleman of the most strict and sacred honor, so there's an end to it! I will not cross furtively tonight as I intended. Should such a man as I flee? Nay, verily. I shall take observations for latitude and longitude tonight, though they may be the last. I feel quite calm now, thank God!'"

■ *God will not necessarily do for us what we can do for ourselves.* The Christian life never lacks in the need for hard work, wisdom and the use of all the skills we have. But, when we do our part, we can be sure God is working in our behalf. Dr. Paul Freed was the founder of TWR, a ministry that beams the gospel throughout the world by radio. In his book *Let The Earth Hear*, Dr. Freed states that "... God can be counted upon to do His part. His part is to direct our creative thinking so that we can become channels of blessing from Him to others."

God will help and direct, but He won't do everything for us. He teams up with us to do His will. We need to work as if everything depended on us and pray as if everything depended on God.

He wants to lead us to the Highway! Isaiah 35 is a promise given to exiled Israel concerning their land. The promise is that they will come back and the land will be reclaimed.

In verses 8-10, Isaiah changes the theme from land to spiritual values and begins to talk about a special highway called the Way of

> "God will help and direct, but He won't do everything for us... We need to work as if everything depended on us and pray as if everything depended on God."

Holiness. These verses describe those who will be and those who will not be on this road.

When I picture this highway, I picture it winding its way through a low lying, swampy, marshy area. The land on which our church now sits was once a low marshy area, and some remember back to the time when they traveled the road in front of the church.

The area on either side was dark and scary, especially to a little child, but the road was elevated high enough for the travelers to remain safe and dry. In the same way, God leads us safely.

He calls us out of the swamps of life, out of spiritual uncleanness and confusion, out of the darkness and guilt of a world without God. He leads us on the Highway of Holiness. F. C. Jennings in his book *Studies in Isaiah* states, "Along that road none unclean can walk; it has no attraction for them; it is for those who have been redeemed and had their sins forgiven."

Furthermore, the Lord Himself is with the travelers to protect them. In fact, Jesus Christ Himself is the Highway. He is the way of Holiness. Christianity is not just following a code of ethics or keeping certain laws. It is a personal relationship with Jesus Christ.

"Years ago a young missionary had to flee from western China. An infuriated mob hotly pursued him. He quickly climbed on a river boat, but the mob followed him there. When he jumped into the river the mob began to throw spears at him. He miraculously escaped unharmed. When he was later telling a friend of the ordeal, a friend asked him,

'What verse from the Bible came to you as you were darting beneath the boat to escape the spears of the mob?' 'Verse?' he asked in astonishment, 'Why, the Lord Himself was with me!'"

We are all born in sin, but when we receive Jesus Christ into our lives we are called Sons of God (John 1:12). Because we are one of His children, our loving heavenly Father gives us His indwelling presence to guide us in all areas of our lives. He will lead us in the ways that are right and Godly.

4

CHAPTER

God Answers Prayer!

"For everyone who asks receives; he who seeks finds; and to him who knocks, the door will be opened."

God promises answers to prayer. Nowhere do the promises of God come more sharply into focus than in the matter of the requests we send to Him. Prayer is our spiritual life line. It is in praying that we connect ourselves with the heart and mind of God. But prayer is not just a one-way street: prayer is two-way communication. We are encouraged to boldly address the God of the universe with our needs and we have a multitude of promises that He will keep.

As an example here is a thrilling incident that happened in a little hut in Africa.

"A missionary was suddenly awakened with a feeling of imminent danger. Fear held her in a vice-like grip. The moon's rays shone through the window, but she could see nothing wrong. She continued to have a feeling of great danger so she woke her husband. They talked in a whisper. Looking beside the bed, they saw a fearsome creature—a giant cobra whose head was raised, ready to strike and inject its venom into the flesh of the missionaries. Quickly the husband reached for his rifle and shot the cobra through its head."

"But the story is not complete. One day while a friend of the missionaries was sweeping the floor in her Canadian town, she had an irresistible urge to pray for these missionaries. 'They are right now in great danger,' she said to herself. So she began to pray. Presently God's peace came into her heart. She knew that God had worked in behalf of her faraway friends. Later, when the missionaries told her of their frightful experience, she compared the date and time of the two experiences. The peril of the missionaries and the burden to pray for them corresponded exactly to the minute."

Answers to prayer are not always visible, but prayer is always answered. This promise is one of the most comforting and supporting in all of Scripture.

Rewards Of Prayer

■ *God wants to give us our desires.* In Luke 11:9-13 and also in Matthew 7:7-12 the same basic message is recorded by the authors. Jesus basically said that if your earthly father knows how to give good gifts to his children *how much more* will your heavenly Father give good gifts to His. He wants to and will give good things to His children in response to their requests.

Prayer links us with the divine. If the channel between the one doing the praying and God is clear and unblocked by sin, what a beautiful opportunity we have to go directly to the throne of grace.

I like to visualize myself standing right in the presence of God presenting my requests just as if I were standing before my earthly father. When I see it in this way I don't have to shout or try some special formula to get His attention. Sometimes I just sit in my chair where I have my devotions and picture God sitting in the chair across from me. It is comforting to think that I am carrying on a conversation with the awesome God who not only is the chief executive officer of the church I pastor, but also Lord of my life.

■ *God has the ability to give us our requests.* In Luke 11 and Matthew 7, the authors record the words of Jesus telling us how much He desires to give us those things that we need. But not only is God wanting to give us what we need, He also is able to accomplish it.

In Numbers 11, the children of Israel were gathered in the wilderness because of their own willful sinfulness. They had not been out of Egypt long before they started to complain about the lack of meat. They focused their frustrations and anger on Moses because of his perceived failures in leadership. As the pressure mounted on Moses, he took this particular need directly to the Lord in prayer. In spite of words of direction from God, Moses began to complain that there simply was not enough food to feed all these people. The interesting interchange is found in Numbers 11:22-23. Moses asked, "'Would they (the people) have enough if flocks and herds were slaughtered for them? Would they have enough if all the fish in the sea were caught for them?' The LORD answered Moses, 'Is the LORD'S arm too short? You will now see whether or not what I say will come true for you.'"

"God not only wants to, but is able to answer our requests."

God told Moses they would have meat. They weren't going to have it for just one day or two days or ten days; they were going to have it for a whole month. In fact they were going to have so much meat that we would say "it will be coming out your ears." God said it would come out their nostrils.

Here was a test of God's ability to do what He said He would do. Moses had difficulty believing this promise. Moses said, "But Lord, there's no way this can happen." Moses, however, was directed to simply tell the people that meat would be provided the next day.

Moses went to the people and told them of God's promise of meat. I don't know whether he told them how much they would get and that it would be coming out their nostrils. That may have been a secret just between him and God.

The next day there came a wind off the sea. The quail began to arrive. The Bible says they came in all around the camp about three feet off the ground (Numbers 11:31). Whether the quail were three feet deep on the ground or they flew in at an altitude of three feet off the ground is not clear. Probably it was the latter. I think it means the quail were close enough so even little children could help their mom and dad gather the meat. It says there was so much quail that no one gathered less than sixty bushels. Now that's a lot of quail. That's enough quail to make you think it's coming out your nose. The Scriptures further add that the quail were gathered on the ground for the distance a person could travel in a day, or about ten miles in every direction.

God had promised to answer the request with meat. When Moses raised his eyebrow in doubt about God's ability to fulfill His promise, the Lord challenged Moses with "Is my arm too short that it can't perform this?" (verse 23). In other words, "Moses, do you think it is impossible for God to do it?"

A rich man took a poor little girl shopping at Christmas time. As they went through the store, he told the little girl she could have anything she wanted. She was shown a $300 doll house, a $200 bike and many other things to delight a young girl's heart. Finally she settled on a $5 stuffed animal. We are surprised and disappointed all at the same time—disappointed that she would not get something that she really wanted and surprised that she did not take advantage of the opportunity. The little girl had limited her choice to what she "thought" she could have. Even though she heard the words that she could have anything she wanted she had always been told "that's too much" or "we can't afford that." She had trouble envisioning anyone having enough money to buy the things that had always been off-limits to her. All her mind could hope for was a $5 stuffed animal. Sometimes our praying is that way: we have very limited vision. We can't comprehend a God who can do more than we can ask or even imagine.

Responsibilities In Prayer

God not only wants to, but is able to answer our requests. He has demonstrated over and over again His ability to do it, but there are some responsibilities we have in prayer. In Luke 18 Jesus taught that it was the responsibility of all men and women to pray. Jesus says in Luke 18:1 that men ought or should always pray and not give up. Then He tells the story of the persistent widow who was insistent that her just request be granted by the unjust judge. Jesus told another story in the same chapter about a man who comes to a friend's home and persistently pleads with his friend to help him with a particular need. After much insistence the friend agrees to help. Jesus told these stories to help the disciples see that they needed to keep on praying and not give up.

The ministries of Jesus were often ushered in by significant seasons of prayer: His baptism, choosing of the twelve disciples, Peter's great confession, and glorification on the Mountain of Transfiguration. How did Jesus pray and how did He teach us to pray? Are there some specific things we can do to make our praying more effective?

■ *Prayers need to be definite.* In Luke 11 the friend said, "Lend me three loaves of bread." One reason our prayers are often mere forms is because they are so general. How many times have we prayed, "Lord bless this group of people or help us in this general area?" The same is true with our blessing at mealtime. We don't try to remember what God has done, so we just make our thanks a

> "When we come to Him we need to believe that He will provide those things for which we pray and request. He will answer."

blanket praise to cover everything. The song writer tried to help us when he wrote, "Count your many blessings, name them one by one and it will surprise you what the Lord has done."

Is there anything specific for which you are praying? Will you be able to tell when it is answered? Will you be able to recognize it? Will you be able to describe how God specifically worked in the matter?

Several years ago I was writing in my journal about my desire to experience more of the Holy Spirit's anointing on my life. I specifically remember being prompted to consider just what that meant. How would I know when it happened? What was I specifically asking the Holy Spirit to do? That prompting caused me to do some thinking. What would I look for? What should I pray for? I wrote down the following things and began to pray for them.

■ *A greater hunger for God!* I wanted an increased desire for God's Word and desire to spend more time in prayer. I particularly wanted to experience an intense yearning for prayer, an increase of my appreciation for the value of prayer and a longing for extended prayer times.

■ *A greater joy in the Lord's work.* I have always loved my work as a pastor, but I sensed it was becoming more mechanical and difficult. I didn't want that. I didn't want to wake up in the morning dreading to go to work another day. I wanted my work to flow out of a heart of love.

■ *A greater joy in the Lord.* I specifically wrote, "I want to be a happier Christian. If I am in a testimony meeting, I don't just want to sit there like so many. I want joy to overflow my soul so that I am immediately ready to give praise. I want to live in that kind of victory."

■ *A greater love for the souls of men.* I wrote in my journal, "When this comes it will be evident in my prayer life, my preaching and my desire for personal evangelism. I, at times, seem more overwhelmed by the mechanics of church work than thinking of souls."

■ *More boldness to witness.* I wanted more boldness without brashness. I prayed that criticism from others would not keep me from personal witness. I wanted to lead more people to Christ in my personal life and not just through the pulpit ministry.

■ *A man of greater faith.* To say with confidence to people, "Stand still and see the salvation of the Lord... God will do it," is what I wanted more of. I wanted more faith.

Even as I am writing this I am marvelling again at how God answered that prayer. It is incredible. I get excited just thinking about it. It was not long after journaling this request that I came into one of the greatest times of prayer and worship I have ever experienced in my life. It was beautiful. The Lord answered this request in detail. I found myself rising at uncommon hours excited about spending time alone with God; knowing more joy in the Lord than ever in all my life; sensing a renewed joy for ministry, caring about the souls of people and making that a priority; praying for and experiencing a greater personal witness; and having a greater sense of faith in my life and work.

■ *We need to be sincere.* Jesus' prayers were warm with feeling. They were expressions of His intense desire for something to happen.

In the same way we need to come to God in sincerity, just as we would to our earthly father. There are times when our children really want something and then there are times when they are just asking for everything on the shelf in the store. At times they are not serious, for they quickly move on to another gift when it appears their original request will not be granted. However, there are other occasions when they keep coming back to the same request. It may be weeks between one inquiry and the next, yet there is that steadiness: "Dad, can I have ....?" A parent finds themselves saying, "They must really want that. It must be important to them. I wonder if there is any way I can get it for them."

God wants to know that we are sincere. We need to regularly, consistently and with full intent of purpose bring our requests to God. It was the strong pleading of the widow before the judge and the persistent knocking and pleading of the friend for loaves of bread that Jesus emphasized in Luke 11.

The story is told of an old blacksmith who hated everything about God and Godliness. He had an opposing argument for anyone who would say anything positive about the Christian faith. A deacon and his wife became deeply distraught because of this blacksmith. One night the two were in prayer concerning this man until the wee hours of the morning. The next morning the deacon went over to the blacksmith's shop and began to talk to the man about the Lord. He responded as usual. Finally the deacon said to him, "My wife and I spent until three in the morning praying for you." At that the deacon broke down and started to cry. He had to terminate his visit and go home. The deacon said to his wife when he got back to his house, "Honey, I blew it. I couldn't share with him." What the deacon and his wife didn't know was that the blacksmith had gone into his own house, began talking to his wife and confessed, "You know I have an argument for everything people can put to me about Christianity, **but I don't have any argument for that kind of compassion and concern."** It was the love and concern of the deacon for this man that was the turning point in the blacksmith's spiritual condition.

■ *Prayers need to exercise faith.* Jesus seemed to indicate in Luke 11 that there were those who were praying and thought God was like some mean old father. Jesus asked: "What father would give a snake to a son who had just asked for something to eat? Or if he asked for breakfast would only offer a stone?"

It would appear there are people who think God is some old sadistic man in the sky who wants to do the opposite of our requests. But that is just not so. Jesus said, "If you being evil know how to give good gifts to your children, how much more does God want to give the good things that you need." When we come to Him we need to believe that He will provide those things for which we pray and request. He will answer. The scriptures are very clear in this area. These things are part of the promises. "Whatever you ask in prayer, believing, you shall have" (Matthew 21:22).

There was one who came to Jesus and said, "If you can, will you please do this for me?" Jesus replied, "It is not a question of whether or not I can. The question is, do you believe I can?"

"Hudson Taylor, great missionary statesman of the past, came to a great crisis in his life at the age of 33 while on a beach on the Southern coast of England. There on a quiet Sunday morning he took a step of faith in response to a simple spiritual principle he had just discovered. He was surprised that this truth had so long eluded him. "If we are obeying the Lord, the responsibility rests with Him, not with us!" Months of struggle were over, and the way ahead was clear. **It was not rash to obey the Scriptures and trust God to be faithful to his pledged Word.** Throwing caution and tradition to the winds, Hudson Taylor formed the China Inland Mission."

Faith will also cause us to make large requests. Too often we only ask that which is little more than what we could do ourselves. We need to ask for such a large request that unless God does something it will not happen.

Michelangelo had a young student named Raphael who had painted a picture on the easel in the studio. Michelangelo came in and noticed that it was scrunched up and cramped in its design. He drew some lines on it and said in bold letters, "AMPLIUS" which meant, enlarge, make it go farther, spread it out.

What if our prayers were painted on a canvas for the Lord to see? Would He write across them "increase, multiply, spread them out, make them larger?" Faith allows us to spread our wings and believe God for greater and greater things, knowing that He longs to answer those prayers.

■ *Prayers need to be persistent.* There are several theories about how long and much we need to pray about any one thing. There are those who say we need not be persistent but merely pray and then claim it. Don't pray about it anymore. In fact these folks would claim it a breach of faith to pray anymore. Still others feel that just the right confession is necessary and the wrong one will give the enemy a foothold that will block the channel of prayer. I believe that Jesus taught us to be persistent when we pray.

Even though the man talked about in Luke 11 doesn't want to get out of bed and get his friend the needed bread, he finally does so because of persistence. His friend keeps knocking. He won't give up. The man in bed is moved by this insistence. I can hear him saying, "Even though the floor is cold and I know I may bother the children, I'll get up and give him the bread." Jesus indicated that's the way He wanted the disciples to pray. Jesus wanted to stress that we should be continually knocking and asking Him for what we feel we need. He wants us to stay at it.

The story of the widow who wanted to receive what was rightly hers from the judge reminds us that we shouldn't give up. This lady persisted in knocking at the judge's door saying, "Give me what I deserve." Finally the judge said, "Because I don't want to suffer a nervous breakdown by her coming to me so much, I will give her what she has coming to her." Jesus commended the lady and said to his disciples, "That's the way I want you to pray. I want you to stay with it; keep on praying."

■ *God answers persistent prayers.* My mother-in-law had several nephews who were not born again. Mom prayed for them regularly. I didn't know how regularly until one of the nephews several years ago came to Christ. This man was in his early 40s when he accepted Christ and it was then that I found out Mom had prayed for him every day for 40 years. I'm sure there were times that she wondered if these prayers would ever be answered, but she kept at it. God rewarded her faithfulness in prayer.

In Matthew 7:7-8 and in Luke 11:9-10, Jesus reminded the disciples again, "I want you to ask and to keep on asking." It is like

> **"Faith allows us to spread our wings and believe God for greater and greater things, knowing that He longs to answer those prayers."**

being a beggar. It indicates total dependency. To paraphrase Jesus, "I want you to ask and those that ask shall receive. Not only do I want you just to ask, but also to knock. For those who knock and keep on knocking, the door will be opened. Furthermore I want you to seek." This word "knock" expresses an urgency about the matter until we find what we are looking for. You notice that these verbs, "ask," "seek" and "knock," increase in intensity. Just think what this means to a God who loves and cares for us.

F. B. Morse, the inventor of the telegraph, was once asked by a pastor the following question: "Prof Morse, when you were making your experiments over in the room at the university, did you ever come to a place of not knowing where to go next?" "Oh yes," he replied, "more than once." "And at such times what then did you do?" To which Prof Morse replied, "I prayed for more light." "And the light generally came?" "When flattering honors came to me from America and Europe on account of the invention that bears my name, I never felt I deserved them. I had made a valuable application of electricity, not because I was superior to other men, but only because God who meant it for mankind must reveal to someone and He was pleased to reveal it to me." It is not surprising the first words sent on the telegraph were "What hath God wrought?"

The greatest prayer that one can ever pray is the one for salvation. I delight in standing before a congregation and saying to them, "If you sincerely ask Jesus to come into your heart I know

He will do it based on the authority and veracity of His Word. The Scriptures remind us, "For whoever shall confess with his mouth the Lord Jesus shall be saved" (Romans 10:9). If we confess in prayer, He forgives.

If you have not prayed to receive Christ, why not do it right now?

5
CHAPTER

So, Why Am I Depressed?

"Be still, and know that I am God; I will be exalted
among the nations, I will be exalted in the earth!"
(Psalms 46:10)

Several years ago I received a phone call from a **distraught person.** The brokenness of the voice at the other end of the line and the unmistakable plea for help reminded me again of the heavy load some carry because of depression. A lackluster marriage, family problems and shattered dreams all contributed to the physical and emotional consequences.

Today's staggering number of suicides and attempted suicides— some estimates run as high as 50-70,000 per year—demonstrates the great need for help in overcoming depression. Further investigation reveals that over half of the population suffers from depression. Some of these people are hospitalized, others are treated as outpatients, while many more go untreated. There are those who believe that depression is at epidemic levels with suicide frequently the outcome. It is a terrible thing to be so depressed that life no longer seems worth living. However, no problem or set of problems is so great that you cannot be helped. Suicide is not the answer. There is hope for you.

We all go through down times. Feelings of depression can be caused by feeling unappreciated, not getting that long awaited job, or getting behind in our bills. If we are further affected by physical problems or lack of rest, things seem much worse. We cannot see the light at the end of the tunnel. Everywhere we look we see only darkness.

I was surprised to find how many of the Biblical characters also went through times of depression. The psalmist in Psalms 42 expressed his problems in the following ways:

"Where can I go meet with God?" *(verse 2b)*

"My tears have been my food day and night..." *(verse 3)*

"Where is your God?" *(verse 3)*

"I used to lead the procession." *(verse 4)*

"Why are you downcast, O my soul?" Why so disturbed within me?" (verse 5)

"My soul is downcast." *(verse 6)*

"I have been swept over by sadness." *(verse 7)*

"I say to God my rock, "Why have you forgotten me?" *(verse 9)*

These are clear signs of depression and despair. The psalmist didn't express much hope of finding a cure for his problems.

Other Biblical characters also expressed moods of depression and some of them quite severe.

Moses: "If this is how you are going to treat me, put me to death right now—if I have found favor in your eyes—and do not let me face my own ruin." (Numbers 11:15)

"... no problem or set of problems is so great that you cannot be helped. Suicide is not the answer. There is hope for you."

Joshua: "Ah, Sovereign Lord, why did you ever bring this people across the Jordan River to deliver us into the hands of the Amorites to destroy us?" (Joshua 7:7) (Note: God never intended Israel to be destroyed, but sin had caused their immediate problem.)

Elijah: "I have had enough, Lord. Take my life; I am no better than my ancestors." (1 Kings 19:4)

Two on the road to Emmaus: "They stood still, their faces downcast." (Luke 24:17)

You may feel very negative about life and do not want to go on. Nothing in your future looks bright. There is nothing exciting to get out of bed for. Each day only brings more pain. You may even feel like you can't go on—like you cannot take even one more minute of life. Such feelings may have been initiated by a bad marriage, a divorce, poor personal relationships, financial difficulties, feelings of inferiority, your job, family problems, physical problems, emotional or physical abuse you suffered, the death of someone very special to you or a variety of other serious problems.

Depression is easy to identify, but how do we get out of it? What does the Bible promise? What are some ways to get out of the pit and back on top?

Get Right With God

This is the first step in helping to solve your problems. You cannot go on to step two until you have successfully completed this one. You must receive Christ as your Savior.

Several weeks ago, a young man walked into my office who was suffering from what I would describe as mild depression. He didn't know what his problem was, but his life was miserable. His marriage wasn't good, he didn't like his work and he didn't like himself, but he didn't know how to improve things.

We talked about some of these areas and then I asked him about his relationship with Christ. Had he asked Christ into his life? He mentioned that he had thought a lot about it and that he wanted to, but he hadn't been able to do it. I explained to him the plan of salvation and then led him in a simple prayer of asking God to forgive his sins and come into his heart.

There were no flashing lights or neon signs, but the next week when he came back for follow up, he said, "I still have some of the same issues to deal with, but they don't seem nearly as great as before." Had all his problems disappeared? No, but he now had an inner power that had not been there before. Jesus Christ had come to take up residence in his life. He was a new creature in Christ Jesus and all things had now become new. He saw things through a new pair of spiritual eyes.

I repeatedly remind our counselors that the only reason our Counseling Center exists is to bring a spiritual emphasis to modern day counseling. There are many good counseling techniques and we need to use the best of them, but counseling will not touch the sin problem that separates one from God. Once we are right with God, we then have His inward presence to help us. Furthermore, we have received His forgiveness.

1 John 1:9 says, "If we confess our sins... He will forgive us our sins and purify us from all unrighteousness."

Romans 8:1 says, "There is now no condemnation for those who are in Christ Jesus."

The relief and release for many from just knowing that their sins are forgiven can put them on the road to recovery. The smile on the face of the young man as he came back to my office during subsequent weeks assured me that his healing had begun. The heavy load of sin was lifted and he now enjoyed "peace with God."

Accept God's Love For You

Rejection is one of the major causes of depression and one of the most negative feelings to overcome. Divorce is particularly damaging to the emotional well being of the participants. In divorce, one spouse may feel rejected and abandoned—traded off for someone else who supposedly has more to offer. This affects a person's self worth, and self esteem. It leaves the abandoned spouse feeling "What is so wrong with me?" and "What more should I have done?"

The psalmist in Psalms 27:9 expresses fears of rejection. David may have penned these words as he was fleeing for his life after the rebellion of his son Absalom and was feeling the pain of being put aside, not only from the people of Israel, but also from members of the royal family. In verse 9 David says, "Do not hide your face from me, do not turn your servant away in anger; ... Do not reject me or forsake me, O God my Savior." He already felt rejected by those closest to him and now he feared God would also reject him.

However, David got back on track and remembered something of the faithfulness of the Lord when he said in verse 10, "Though my father and mother forsake me, the Lord will receive me." David knew enough about God to know that under no circumstances would God forsake him. At no time would he ever be out from under the watchful and caring eye of the Lord.

You may feel like everyone has rejected you, but I want to assure you that God has not abandoned you. You may be going through a testing time; Satan may be trying to "sift" you like he did Peter, and you may feel like no one cares, but God does. He reminds us in Hebrews 13:5 that "Never will I leave you; never will I forsake you."

Keep reminding yourself that God loves you and cares for you even if you don't, at first, feel that it is true. You may not see or understand what God is doing or believe that good can ever come out of your circumstances, but God is true to His Word and has promised to never leave you. If you continue to abide in Him, you are constantly under the protective shadow of the Almighty.

God further shows His love by constantly surrounding us with spiritual assistants called angels. Hebrews 1:14 says that **all angels are "ministering spirits sent to serve those who will inherit salvation."** We don't know much about how angels work, but we find them used frequently in the Bible to help the people of God at difficult times in their lives. Psalms 91:11 says "For He (God) will command his angels concerning you to guard you in all your ways." God sent an angel to shut the lion's mouth, protecting Daniel (Daniel 6:22). Angels came to Peter to help him escape from jail (Acts 12:7-10) and later to Paul to reassure him that all the crewmen would be rescued in the coming shipwreck (Acts 27:23-26). When Jesus was praying on the Mount of Olives during the night of His arrest, Luke 22:43 tells us that "an angel appeared to Him and strengthened Him." Jesus later reminded Peter, after Peter had taken up the sword to defend Jesus, that He could call on His Father and "He will at once put at my disposal more than twelve legions of angels" (Matthew 26:53). My friend, you are not alone. Your rejection may have led to severe depression, but begin to think about the presence of God and the great heavenly host with the task of caring for God's children.

Wait Patiently For God To Act

If you are right with God and can at least mentally accept that God loves you and is working on your behalf, then you have the foundation for confidence in knowing that God does know about your problem and is working out His will in your life. However, it is not always easy to wait. We want instant answers to our problems. Moses must have been impatient when he saw the Red Sea in front of him and the Egyptian Army pursuing him from the back, but the Lord convinced him to tell the people of Israel, "Do not be afraid, stand firm and you will see the deliverance the Lord will bring you today." (Exodus 14:13). Moses had every human right to be depressed. The people he was leading were bitterly complaining about some of the decisions he had made, but God was there to help him through the waters. One of my favorite verses is Psalms

> **"... While you are waiting for God to act in the major way you desire, there are other things you can be doing to help your situation. Remember to hustle while you wait."**

46:10, "Be still, and know that I am God; I will be exalted among the nations, I will be exalted in the earth!" I have often quoted that verse to myself as a reminder to be still, stop talking and listen to God speak.

Several years ago I was going through a difficult time with several perplexing problems facing me that I was not able to solve by my human ingenuity. It was then that I discovered the rest of Psalms 46:10. I was reminded that I was to be still or patient and watch God work. In the ensuing verses, God stated he would be "exalted among the nations and in the earth." His power and wisdom would work out a solution that would make my puny efforts seem pale in comparison. God wanted to do it in His way and in His time. He wanted me to stop my fretting and worrying. I have not perfected such watching, but I am working on it and it is thrilling to experience. However, such "waiting" does not imply idleness.

Idleness for the depressed person can drive the depression even deeper. If you are depressed you may not feel like doing anything. However, you need to be active so that your mind thinks about things other than your depression and to help your body get tired out so sleep will come more naturally.

You may wonder how I can suggest activity when I have just suggested that patience is a virtue. Let me illustrate. Several years ago we were in the process of planning for a major building program at our church. Things were not going as quickly as I wanted them to. I was expressing to our Planning Committee my disappointment about a major delay when a dear brother in the Lord said, "Pastor, we can still hustle while we wait." I had never heard that expression before, but simply put, it meant there were other things we could be doing until we could begin actual construction. The delay did not have to mean wasted time. While you are waiting for God to act in the major way you desire, there are other things you can be doing to help your situation. Paul had to remind the Christians at Thessalonica that even while they waited for the coming of the Lord they were not to be idle. They were to be busily working with their hands and earning their keep (2 Thessalonians 3:6-13).

■ *Keep busy until the Lord brings you the answer to your situation.* Don't sit at home every day and have a pity party. Plan a routine and follow it. If people ask you to go out to eat with them, do it. Take up a volunteer job at the hospital or the church if other full time employment does not appeal to you. Many churches could give someone significant full time work if they would only volunteer. By volunteering, you may not only help yourself, but also the Lord's work. Remember to "hustle while you wait."

Praise God Even In The Difficult Times

This is one of the most difficult steps, yet one of the most rewarding. We all agree that it is easy to praise God when everything is going smoothly and we have no major cares. It is quite another thing to praise Him when we are going through a dark valley. However, the ability to praise Him in the dark valleys is evidence of strong Christian faith.

Habakkuk, the prophet, faced extreme difficulties and then penned one of the most beautiful passages in the Bible. Habakkuk began his book by complaining to God about all the wickedness he saw in Israel. He expressed signs of depression by asking "God, where are you?" ... "Aren't you hearing my cry?" ... "How long must I call for help before you answer me?" God then responded to him in Habakkuk 1:5-6 by telling him that He was raising up the Babylonians to bring judgement on Israel. These were words that Habakkuk did not want to hear. Why would God use a people more wicked than Israel to bring judgement? Habakkuk couldn't come up with any satisfactory answers. He couldn't figure it out. In 2:1 Habakkuk grew silent before the Lord. He was waiting to see what God was going to say. God did not give a complete answer, but He did want Habakkuk to simply trust Him to work it out. He reminds him that the "righteous will live by faith." Habakkuk was to be patient and have faith in God, even though Habakkuk did not fully understand what God was doing. Then in chapter 3, Habakkuk progresses to the point where he is able to praise the Lord in spite of the difficult times he saw coming on Israel.

Do You See the Progression in Habakkuk's Healing?

■ *Step 1: Habakkuk was very depressed and bitter* in Chapter 1 about what he feels is God's inattention to his pleas for help. Then, when God did answer, he didn't like what God had to say.

Have you ever felt like Habakkuk? Maybe you feel that way right now? If so, please read on to see how you can move to the next step of healing.

■ *Step 2: Habakkuk began to walk by faith.* He still didn't like what he saw, but you sense more of a steadiness in Habakkuk's spirit in chapter 2. God began to show him that even though He will use the hated and cruel Babylonians to bring judgement, the knowledge of the Lord will still cover the earth (2:14) and that the Lord was still in charge of all things. In the light of that truth, all the earth should be silent before Him (2:20). Habakkuk developed a new appreciation for God's knowledge of the situation. He came to acknowledge that "God does know what is going on" and concluded that he had better stop his complaining.

■ *Step 3: Habakkuk is able to praise the Lord even if everything goes bad.* This third step is by far the most difficult, but it is the sign of true healing. His words of testimony in 3:17-19 are some of the greatest in Scripture. In verse 17 he describes how bad the situation could get when he says, "Though the fig tree does not bud and there are no grapes on the vines, though the olive crop fails and the fields produce no food, though there are no sheep in the pen and no cattle in the stalls." There can't be a future much more dismal than that. For an agricultural society, it meant everything was failing. It was total economic disaster. This meant starvation and ruin.

However, Habakkuk had gotten to the point where he could go on to say, "Yet I will rejoice in the Lord, I will be joyful in God my Savior."

How had he been able to make the transition from a "complainer" in Step 1 to that of a "praiser" in Step 3? He knew that God was well aware of all his problems and would give him whatever strength he needed for whatever situation he faced. He also knew that God would give Him more than enough help to climb above the surface conflicts.

Friend, at what stage of healing are you? If you are in stage 1, why not ask God to help you to go to stage 2 where you begin to trust Him with your difficulties? If you are in stage 2, take the next step and begin to praise Him for His unlimited ability, not only to work out His will perfectly, but also to help you become an overcomer.

Other Helpful Steps In The Healing Process

Practice Forgiveness

Have you ever listened to the recorded music and messages played in some stores? If you listen carefully you will notice the music and message begin to repeat after a period of time. This recurrent, continuous play is achieved by a tape loop. The music and message is recorded on a length of tape with the beginning and end joined, resulting in a continuous audio message or loop.

Some people regularly experience a similar phenomena. They play a mental loop in their mind of an event that reminds them of a mistake or unhappy event that haunts them. Perhaps their mental loop is a fantasy of horror or pleasure that they would never admit to another person. This mental loop has a way of exercising a control over them they may not realize or truly want. Experiences of the past have a way of affecting our future. We can develop deep fears and anxieties that restrict our ability to function freely and happily, as God intended. Worse yet are those un-Godly thoughts a person may harbor that lead him away from the pure and wholesome thoughts that serve to build up a person.

Jesus Christ came to break the destructive mental loop and to replace it with one that is more edifying. Do not be deceived, there is one who sees every un-Godly thought. And He can help you reject it and replace it with better thoughts and make you a better person. There is no sin in our past that Jesus cannot forgive and no hurt He cannot heal.

Do you feel like you have been wronged? Do you wake up reliving the neglect, mistreatment, or abuse you have experienced? Do you find your mind playing the "same tape" over and over again day after day? If such is the case, your healing will be complete only as you learn to forgive those whom you feel have wronged you. You may choose to live in self-pity and anger, but God has called us to a different life. A grudge is one thing that won't get better by nursing it. **Forgiveness is not natural or easy and can only be truly accomplished with God's help.**

First, forgiveness is an act of our will. It is something we choose to do or not to do. You cannot change the way people have treated you but you can choose to forgive them for the way they have treated you. You don't have to let it eat you up. The manner of your forgiveness is to be in the same way that Christ forgave us.

Have you ever struggled with forgiving someone for something they may have said about you or done to you? Others have told you to forget it and go on but for some reason it is just not that easy for you?

A lot of old church buildings have a tower that encloses a large bell. Somewhere in the foyer of that building is a large rope attached to the bell. I have often observed the bell ringer of a particular church get a hold of that rope and begin to pull. At first it seemed he had to work quite hard to get the bell moving but once he got it moving it wasn't that hard to maintain the momentum. The bell continued to ring easily.

The ringing bell is like our unforgiving spirit. Once we get it in motion it continues to stay in motion with little effort. When we give a little tug on the rope of our memories, that unforgiving spirit rings loud and clear and the spirit of anger and bitterness again wells up within us. But, how do we stop this madness?

Corrie Ten Boom who spent a number of years in a German concentration camp likened forgiveness to letting go of the bell rope. She advised people to take their hands off the rope—to refuse to keep ringing the bell. Eventually the bell will come to a halt. And in a similar manner if we cease rehearsing the injustices done to us and let go of them, the unforgiving spirit will subside. **Forgiveness is something you do and not just something you feel.** But what sweet relief we find as we forgive others.

Second, forgiveness is a Christian action. I previously mentioned that forgiveness is not normal for the nonbeliever. The natural reaction when we have been wronged is to want to "get even" or "get revenge"; therefore, to truly forgive is a divine act. Such action must come from "agape" love that only comes from a relationship with the Lord Jesus Christ.

Sometimes Christians don't overtly try to get even, but we do internalize all the injustices done to us and let them eat at us. We feel it is not right to lash back at someone or verbalize our true feelings so we just bottle it up and let it be the seed bed for depression. We need to admit our anger and resentment, seek for forgiveness from God and others and plead for God's love to rule in our hearts.

Divine peace is the result of seeking forgiveness. You won't always feel like seeking forgiveness or forgiving someone, but when you choose to do it because it is a Christian act, then God will come to your rescue and grant you His peace and inner joy as well as answering your prayer. I have seen this work time and time again in marriages where at least one of the partners was Christian. In a number of cases the one spouse had every reason to walk away from the marriage and no one would have faulted them. Instead they stayed, and demonstrated Christian love and forgiveness. Some of those homes have turned into beautiful Christian families.

A believer cannot go on living a life of anger, bitterness and resentment against others. Even though you think the other person should make the first move to come to you, you need to start the ball rolling and go to them. They may not even be aware that you feel they have wronged you. God will help you and bring a wonderful sense of healing to you.

Walk In The Spirit

If the Spirit of God dwells in us, He will be producing characteristics in our lives that are like Christ. It is a natural outcome of letting Him lead us. The characteristics of the Spirit that should be growing and maturing in our lives are "love, joy, peace, patience, kindness, goodness, faithfulness, gentleness and self-control" (Galatians 5:22-23). In a state of deep depression, you may not feel like manifesting these values, but I ask you to stop right now and ask the Holy Spirit to help you. Tell Him you want to do what's right and ask Him to show you specifically where you can begin to change. It may be in the way you treat your children or the tone of voice you use with your co-workers. Whatever the Spirit says to you, do it.

Meditate Daily On The Word

Depression is primarily a condition of the mind and spirit of man, which can be complicated by a physical condition. Therefore, what we feed our minds is very important. To saturate our minds with Scripture is more than just creating a positive mental attitude. The Word of God is powerful. The Scripture describes itself as a devouring flame (Jeremiah 5:14), a crushing hammer (Jeremiah 23:29), a life-giving force (Ezekiel 37:7), a saving power (Romans 1:16), a defensive weapon (Ephesians 6:17), and a probing instrument (Hebrews 4:12). It was also written to give us hope for the future. Romans 15:4 says "For everything that was written in the past was written to teach us, so that through endurance and the encouragement of the Scriptures we might have hope." When we read the Scriptures, meditate on them and memorize them, something uniquely powerful happens in our lives. The same power that brings conviction to the sinner can bring hope to the depressed.

I never fully appreciated the power of the Word until one time I was in a room with a demon possessed person and the Word was used to confront the demons speaking through that individual. The possessed person cowered in fear as the Word was read. It was an awesome scene I will never forget. Since then I have had a new respect for the power of the Word whenever it is read in public or private. I try to imagine the wonderful things that happen in the lives of people sitting in my congregation when it is time for the weekly Scripture reading. That same power is available to you. You may not be able to read a lot at first but concentrate on what you do read. Find meaningful passages that fit your needs. Notice words of encouragement and promise. If you will believe the Scriptures, God will make His truth real to you.

You do not have to live in a perpetual state of depression. God desires your life to be abundant and joyful. Christ even prayed that the joy He had might be in His followers. This joy is not a frivolous joy, but a deeply satisfying and peaceful one that is ours in spite of difficulties. You too can experience that joy if you are right with God, accept His love, wait patiently for God to act, practice forgiveness, walk in the Spirit, and meditate daily on His Word. You can say with the prophet Habakkuk, "The Sovereign Lord is my strength; he makes my feet like the feet of a deer; he enables me to go on the heights." (Habakkuk 3:19)

6
CHAPTER

Finding The Hurricane's Eye

*"You will keep in perfect peace him whose
mind is steadfast, because he trusts in you."
(Isaiah 26:3)*

A Canadian pastor, in a period of great despondency, received the help he needed from reading the following delightful true incident. The local parks commission had been ordered to remove the trees from a certain street which was to be widened. As they were about to begin, the foreman and his men noticed a robin's nest in one of the trees and the mother robin sitting on the nest. The foreman ordered the men to leave the tree until later. Returning, they found the nest occupied by little wide-mouthed robins. Again they left the tree. When they returned at a later date they found the nest empty. The family had grown and flown away. But something woven into the bottom of the nest caught the eye of one of the workmen, a soiled little white card. When he separated it from the mud and sticks, he found that it was a small Sunday school card and on it the words, "We trust in the Lord our God."

Jesus shared an illustration about how the little birds are cared for by our loving heavenly Father and then He added these words, "Are you not much more valuable than they?" (Matthew 6:26). We too often worry and fret about life's uncertainties and it robs us of much of the joy and rest we could be experiencing. All the while God wants us to place our trust in Him. The Scripture reminds us to "cast all our cares on Him for He cares for us" (1 Peter 5:7).

We live in a fast paced world. Many people are exhausted at day's end. They drop into the easy chair and before long have drifted off to sleep. They rise in the morning nearly as tired as when they went to bed. Why? Should not a night of sleeping get a person in better shape than that? Still others come home exhausted physically, but are not able to go to sleep: their mind will not slow down enough to let the body rest. For still others there is a lack of inner peace that keeps life in turmoil. Trying to run through waist high water or sloshing through deep mud is what it is like for some to get through life. They are quickly exhausted and worn out from a life that is not peaceful. There is so much mental and emotional strain that they are exhausted just thinking about their circumstances.

There are possible physical ailments that can cause some of these problems and they should certainly be treated. However, problems of the spirit, emotions, and attitude also have a profound effect on a person's energy level and outlook.

Ideally, the life of the Christian should be one that is more restful, calm, and reposed. Agitation, worry and fretfulness should not continually plague the normal child of God. The Scriptures repeatedly promise us rest. Throughout the Old Testament and into the New Testament there are various Scriptures that talk of rest.

It is promised for all phases and seasons of a person's life.

Just listen to a few passages of scripture on this subject:

"My soul finds rest in God alone; my salvation comes from him." (Psalms 62:1)

"He who dwells in the shelter of the Most High will rest in the shadow of the Almighty." (Psalms 91:1)

"This is what the Sovereign LORD, the Holy One of Israel, says: 'In repentance and rest is your salvation, in quietness and trust is your strength.'" (Isaiah 30:15)

"This is what the LORD says: 'Stand at the crossroads and look; ask for the ancient paths, ask where the good way is, and walk in it, and you will find rest for your souls.'" (Jeremiah 6:16)

"Come to me, all you who are weary and burdened, and I will give you rest." (Matthew 11:28)

"There remains, then, a Sabbath-rest for the people of God." (Hebrews 4:9)

Psalms 40 opens with a very precarious position that is anything but restful. The Psalmist is in a slimy pit where there is no sure footing. This may be a pit that has no bottom and that will eventually become his grave. Or it may be a pit that is simply slippery and filled with waist high muck and mire. The footing is very unstable. I picture it like climbing a slippery slide in the school playground. Even the best of shoes cannot grip the metal that has been polished by the scores of bodies that have gone down it.

What was it that caused this man to describe his situation as a slimy pit? Was it a descriptive picture of sin and the consequences of such a life? Possibly. For sin indeed places us in a precarious spot where we stumble and fall. There is no sure footing and the end is death. Was the Psalmist suggesting a picture of a troubled soul that is beset with tremendous feelings of fear and insecurity because of a troubled inner being? That too may be the situation that prompted David to write as he did. But rather than focus on what the pit was like, let's see what David experienced in his exit from the pit.

Notice how he describes his escape in Psalms 40:2-3:

"He lifted me out of the slimy pit, out of the mud and mire; he set my feet on a rock and gave me a firm place to stand. He put a new song in my mouth, a hymn of praise to our God."

David was spiritually and emotionally exhilarated as he described what happened to him. He was resting like never before. Solid footing, a new song and a heart of praise do much to lighten the soul.

There are different types of stressful situations. There are situations where you can bring about change, but are not sure what to do. There are other stressful situations when you are not able to do anything at all. There's no move you can make. The situation is simply there and it's a stressful one. At other times you may have reached the limit of your endurance. It seems as though all of your strength is gone. You simply aren't able to go on. You're exhausted. Is there any help for these situations?

There Is Rest Because He Promised It

"Come to me, all you who are weary and burdened, and I will give you rest" (Matthew 11:28). Paul in 2 Corinthians 1 wrote about a bad situation he had found in Asia, which was stressful to his soul. He said it was so bad that it seemed he had the sentence of death on his heart. He was under great pressure far beyond his ability to endure. "But this happened that we might not rely on ourselves but upon God ... On Him we have set our hope that He will continue to deliver us." (2 Corinthians 1:9-10)

Some of you have been to the point where adequate strength was not in yourself—it was in Him. You said, "No longer can I do it God, I'm now resting my whole future on you."

I look forward every summer to at least a week of vacation at a friend's cabin at beautiful Higgins Lake in the northern portion of Michigan's lower peninsular. This is a wonderful location for renewing my spiritual batteries and getting rested up from being in the battle. I need these times of refreshing in part because of my

> "Ideally, the
> life of the
> Christian
> should be one
> that is more
> restful, calm,
> and reposed."

nature. I am a doer and feel that if things are going to happen it depends on me. I'm not concerned that God will be sitting on His hands, but I do get concerned that I might not be doing what I'm supposed to be doing. As a result, I tend to carry more stress than I should and that makes life less restful than necessary. One summer I was particularly stressed. The load had been heavy and you know what that can do to one's spirit. For my devotions that vacation I was reading in Isaiah. I had read the book many times before, but this time a verse jumped out at me that became my theme verse for the next several years. I found myself giving the verse to people who were going through similar situations. It became a regular source of inspiration.

God said to Israel through the prophet Isaiah, "In repentance and rest is your salvation, in quietness and trust is your strength, but you would have none of it." (Isaiah 30:15). Israel was facing formidable opposition from outside enemies and the course of action chosen by the nation was one of "rugged individualism"—a "we can do it by ourselves" mentality. But God wanted them to come to Him for help. He wanted them to turn from their sin and let Him provide deliverance.

As I read that passage I thought some of it fit me. My spirit had not been particularly quiet which in turn had sapped my inner strength and energy. God was concerned about me. He wanted me to look more to Him. I felt God was leading me to let Him take more of the load and rest in His provisions. He had an endless supply of energy and could move things in minutes that I couldn't move in years. I found a new joy in service and a renewed sense of peace and rest from accepting the promise.

In the Book of Common Prayer, Matthew 11:28 reads, "Come

unto me all ye that travail and are heavy laden and I will refresh you." Matthew 11:29 says, "Take my yoke upon you and learn from me, for I am gentle and humble in heart, and you will find rest for your souls." This is an interesting verse especially when compared to verse 28. In verse 28 God gives us a gift if we come to Him. But in verse 29 we are to take His yoke upon us. A yoke is something that was put across the necks of a team oxen to help them work together when pulling various types of heavy loads. When we take His yoke we make a discovery: His yoke is easy, His burden is light, and we find rest. For those who come to Christ there is rest. For those who take His yoke it implies a deep abiding and permanent repose—undisturbed in the turmoil of living.

In 2 Corinthians 12, Paul asks God three times to take away some form of suffering. We are not told what it was. In verse 9 Paul is reminded that Christ's grace would be sufficient and that Christ's power was perfected in Paul's weakness.

When the 10 plagues came to Egypt, it was not something the children of Israel caused or even something that Moses thought up. In this case, God took over and caused the plagues so He could bring the Israelites out by His own hand.

The children of Israel had left Egypt in Exodus 14 and now found themselves between the Red Sea and the Egyptian Army. Moses was in "hot water" because of the situation. The people were grumbling and complaining, asking why they had let Moses lead them there in the first place. "Why weren't we allowed to die in Egypt?" Now friends, if I had been Moses, I would have been stressed. I would probably have been in bad shape emotionally. Moses asked the people to just relax, rest and stand firm and see the salvation of the Lord. There was nothing the Israelites could do about the situation, but stand there. God was going to have to make things happen if they were to survive. God said He would defend and protect them and He did. When they stood firm He opened up the Red Sea and they went through on dry ground. They were stressed, but they rested upon God. We also can rest because He promised it.

We Can Rest Because Of His Presence

In Exodus 33:14-15 it is written, "The LORD replied, 'My Presence will go with you, and I will give you rest.' Then Moses said to him, 'If your Presence does not go with us, do not send us up from here.'" Just the fact that God is with us gives us rest. In Psalms 23 David wrote, "He makes me lie down, He leads me, He restores me, He leads in right paths and He is the one who goes through the valley of death with me. I rest because He is there." The Psalmist furthermore states: "He who dwells in the shelter of the Most High will rest in the shadow of the Almighty. I will say of the LORD, "He is my refuge and my fortress, my God, in whom I trust." (Psalms 91:1-2)

As a young boy I delivered morning papers. On those dark still mornings I could become engulfed with fear if I wasn't careful. I remember riding my bike or walking under one of the dimly lit street lights and all of a sudden seeing this thing dart out in front of me, off to my side, or from behind me. More than once, it startled me and kept me looking back. Then I realized it was my shadow.

While I didn't always like seeing my shadow at that time of the morning I learned an important lesson: the shadow is never far away from the object casting it.

If we are resting in the shadow of the Most High—He is not far away. The shadow indicates His presence.

> Ira Sankey, great song evangelist of the last century, was aboard a ship and was requested to sing a hymn. He sang "Savior, like a shepherd lead us how we need thy tender care..."
>
> After he finished the song a gentleman came up to him and asked, "Were you in the Union Army?"
>
> "I was," Sankey replied.
>
> "Were you in the army in the spring of 1860?"
>
> "I was."
>
> "Do you remember doing picket duty one particular moonlit night?"

"Yes, I remember that night!"

The other fellow said, "I was in the Confederate Army and I was hiding in the bushes. I had lifted my musket and had my finger on the trigger and was ready to take your life. Then I noticed you closed your eyes and lifted your head heavenward and began to sing a song. There was something in me that said, 'I've got all kinds of time to take his life, I'm going to listen to his song and then I'll shoot him." He went on to remind Sankey that he had sung that same hymn as the one on the ship. "When you came to the part about 'we are Thine do Thou befriend us, be the guardian of our way...,' it triggered in my memory things about my Godly Mother. She used to always sing that song and I don't know whether it was the hand of God or something else, but I think it was God who was the guardian of your way and caused me to take my finger off the trigger and drop my gun."

Because of His presence we can rest.

We Can Rest Because Of His Peace

As Jesus was preparing to leave this earth, He told His disciples that He didn't want them to have a troubled and agitated heart. He promised to come back and take them with Him. He also told them He wanted to give them His peace. He didn't want the events in the world to get them all troubled (John 14:1-27).

Other promises of rest are provided in God's Word where it says, "You will keep in perfect peace him whose mind is steadfast because he trusts in you" (Isaiah 26:3) and "my God will meet all your needs according to his glorious riches in Christ Jesus" (Philippians 4:19).

The Psalmist found it peaceful and restful in his new experience with God and declares in Psalms 40:3, "He put a new song in my mouth, a hymn of praise to our God." Is it not a puzzle to you that many people think religion is gloom, doom and sadness? In fact salvation produces just the opposite.

The Bible is a book of songs. In the book of Revelation there is more singing than pronouncement of woes. There is coming judgment, woes and terrible things on the earth but while Revelation lists nine woes it also records ten different songs sung by eight different choirs. When God was establishing the worship in the temple He said he wanted some of the Levites to do nothing but be involved in the music ministry of the temple. In re-reading the Christmas story you will discover that nowhere did the angels sing to the shepherds—they only spoke their message with excitement. Some have suggested the lack of singing by the angels is because singing and songs are only for the "redeemed."

Revelation 5:9 says, "And they sang a new song: 'You are worthy to take the scroll and to open its seals, because you were slain, and with your blood you purchased men for God from every tribe and language and people and nation.'"

The Apostle John writes in Revelation 14:3 "And they sang a new song before the throne and before the four living creatures and the elders. No one could learn the song except the 144,000 who had been redeemed from the earth."

He has promised us songs in the night, songs during the dark times of life, songs when it seems there is no way out and the burdens are so great. In the worst times of our lives He can give us a song.

Psalms 42:8 says, "By day the LORD directs his love, at night his song is with me—a prayer to the God of my life."

Paul and Silas were falsely accused and beaten as Luke records for us in Acts 16:25: "About midnight Paul and Silas were praying and singing hymns to God, and the other prisoners were listening to them."

The great hymn "It Is Well With My Soul" was written after the author had lost his entire family, except his wife, in a tragedy at sea. It was a time of great sorrow. In spite of that he still spoke of peace when he wrote "when sorrow like sea billows roll, whatever my lot thou hast taught me to say, it is well, it is well with my soul."

We Can Rest Because We Are Redeemed

Unless Christ returns during your lifetime, life as you know it now is still terminal. If we live to be 120 years old and then die, it is still temporary. But Christ has given you a great hope that is a constant source of rest and encouragement.

"There remains, then, a Sabbath—rest for the people of God;" (Hebrews 4:9).

"Let us, therefore, make every effort to enter that rest, so that no one will fall by following their example of disobedience. (Hebrews 4:11).

"Then I heard a voice from heaven say, 'Write: Blessed are the dead who die in the Lord from now on.' 'Yes,' says the Spirit, 'they will rest from their labor, for their deeds will follow them.'" (Revelation 14:13).

I have quoted this last verse hundreds of times as I have stood by the grave side or in the chapel at the cemetery and delivered a committal message. For the child of God there is an eternal rest. There is hope for the believer that as soon as we leave this body we enter immediately into the presence of God. We enter our home of eternal bliss. If the new Jerusalem described in Revelation 21-22 is what our eternal home will be like, and we believe it is, then all of earth's labors and toils will quickly vanish from our thinking when we enter our final rest.

The man in the slippery slimy pit is like a person without Christ. The prophet Isaiah described a person without God "like the tossing sea, which cannot rest, whose waves cast up mire and mud" (Isaiah 57:20). Such a person doesn't know the joy of salvation: he doesn't have a song of hope in his heart nor a restful spirit. As terrible as this condition is, there is still hope.

God wants to put you on a solid foundation. He wants to put a new song in your heart and give you hope and rest. If you will invite Christ into your heart you will find a peace and joy that brings you a rest that you never thought possible. Why not confess your sins and open the door of your life to Him right now?

7
CHAPTER

Fresh Starts For Stale Lives

"I live in a high and holy place,
but also with him who is contrite and lowly in spirit,
to revive the spirit of the lowly and
to revive the heart of the contrite."
(Isaiah 57:15)

When we think of revivals we often think in terms of the great Welsh Revival in Britain, or revivals during the early days of our new nation under the leadership of men like George Whitfield, John Wesley and Jonathan Edwards, the Midwest revivals of the late 1800s under the preaching of Charles G. Finney, the Azusa Street revival of the early 1900s, or the Asbury Revival during the late 1960s to the early 1970s. We think of revival as being those times when it seems God sovereignly moves into a church or community and just literally takes control of the situation. Or when people are overwhelmed with a sense of the holiness of God, their own sinfulness, and the great need for repentance.

It was reported that when Jonathan Edwards preached his most famous sermon, "Sinners in the Hands of An Angry God," that some people fell in the aisles under deep conviction while others held on to the pew and begged him to stop for they could not take anymore conviction. What makes this report even more remarkable is that Jonathan Edwards had such poor eyesight that he had to hold his manuscript just inches from his face as he spoke in a rather monotonous voice. It seems that the sovereign moving of the Spirit of God came in such power that people were supernaturally moved in their feeling toward God and relationship with Him.

To read about such powerful movements is both exciting and challenging. I have often longed to be in such a place and see first hand what so far I have only read about in books or heard others tell about. Oh, I have been in some wonderful services and have seen people weep over the conviction of sin, have sensed the powerful hand of God to bring hope to the hopeless and to wonderfully deliver others from a terrible life of sin. I still long to see such a wide sweeping, non-orchestrated, sovereign movement of God on a church, city or nation of which I am a part. What am I to do in the meantime? What are the Biblical directives? What has God promised about revival? What are His people to do?

God does promise revival to those who seek Him even if it is only on an individual basis. We don't need to go through life dried up spiritually like an old prune. We don't need to feel parched like the desert that calls for the cool refreshing spring. We don't have to fight every day just to get a little spiritual energy to read a few verses of Scripture.

We can be a well watered plain of spiritual soil that not only provides us with nourishment, but is also a blessing to others. We can be leaders in spiritual growth. A vibrant and consistent spiritual walk with the Lord is to be the norm rather than the exception.

"We don't need to go through life dried up spiritually like an old prune."

Times of revival are usually necessary for both individuals and nations. It is not the nature of man to perpetually live on the mountain top of spiritual experience. At some point the spiritual fervor begins to wane and he moves from the heartwarming and highly emotional experience to one that is routine, deliberate, mundane and dry. When it is only habit or routine that drives a person spiritually and one has lost his spiritual fervor, then it is time for revival. Such people are in need of being awakened and renewed. The first love needs to be restored. The Apostle John spoke about such a need while writing to the church at Ephesus. They too had left their first love.

By many standards used today, the Ephesian church described in Revelation 2:1-7 would have been a wonderfully successful church. They were a church that was accustomed to hard work, they sought to be separate from worldly practices, purity of thought and life were important to them and they sought to maintain a doctrinally sound church. For these things they were commended by both their peers and God. I can only imagine how excited and proud the church leaders felt as they prepared to go to their annual church conference and give reports of how they had stood faithful, how they handled a certain false prophet and how they dealt with other difficult persons. But in all their commendations there was something that Christ was not pleased with. They had forsaken their first love.

What is our first love? Why was it so important to Christ and what does it mean to us?

I remember going to a Bethel College youth convention during my senior year in high school. I looked across the gym and saw the most beautiful girl I had ever seen. Wow—I liked what I saw. I made a commitment to meet her before I left Bethel that weekend. Her cousin was also there for the weekend so I got him to introduce us. I remember talking to her for the first time while standing in the foyer of the girls' dorm. There was this special tingle that I experienced in my heart as I left the lobby of the dorm that day. It followed me as I sat through the next meeting and even as I looked back into the room to see if she was still there. It stayed with me after I returned to my home.

Even though I lived 250 miles from her, I can still remember getting off the school bus thinking about her. After a month of such emotional feelings I tried to write her. It was an effort because I didn't know what to say. Finally I got my older brother to help me compose the letter. That first important letter was less than a small stationery-size page. She got it on her 16th birthday and just after she had broken up with another fellow.

I was working on a farm at the time I sent the letter. Whenever I would be in town delivering grain to the elevator, I would drive by my house to see if the mail had arrived, particularly any letters with a certain return address. Finally the day arrived when I got the special letter. I took it in the truck with me just to smell the perfume and have it with me so I could read it again and again and again. That began a correspondence that lasted the remainder of our senior year. We both enrolled at Bethel to pursue our college education. We dated regularly and were married three years later. That special girl is now Margaret my wife.

There was and is a special "something" I have with Margaret that I have never had with anyone else.

I love my parents and siblings, but it isn't like this. I love the people of my congregation and look forward to being with them, but it isn't the same as my relationship with Margaret. She is my first love. She is the love of my earthly life. When I come home from a trip, she is the first one I look for as I come down the walk way. She is the one I look forward to going home to see each evening. We laugh together. She even laughs at my jokes and the "funny" things I do or say when no one else thinks they're funny. There is nothing like that first love.

Jesus said to the church at Ephesus that even though they were doing many good things they had lost their first love. This was a church that had fallen in love with Jesus Christ and were zealous to defend the faith and contend for sound doctrine, but their love for Christ had turned into cold, lifeless duty rather than exciting and joyous service.

Here we have the picture of a husband and wife living in the same house, but not having a home. They are only going through the motions of being husband and wife. She does the laundry, gets the meals in the evening and cleans the house. He trims the shrubs, feels the responsibility to provide for the family and takes care of the cars. But there is little love between the two. They have a piece of paper that says they are married, they share the same name, care for the children and put food on the table, but the love that ought to bond their marriage is lacking.

That's what Ephesus was like and that's what a lot of people and churches are like as well. Individuals or churches who have lost their first love and are in need of revival have some of the following characteristics:

■ *More form than feeling* They know the right words, when to sit and stand and how to say the liturgy, but the heart warming love for Christ that should move and motivate them is missing.

■ *More "letter of the law" than "spirit of the law"* Their relationships with others are often governed by legalism, a critical spirit, and a feeling of superiority. They are harsh and cynical if things in the church are not done the way they have always been done. Any new forms or approaches are suspect and questionable. Someone has said, "some people are as straight as a gun barrel and just as empty." I would add "and just as cold."

■ *Equate "busy-ness" with love for Christ* They are so busy "doing" good things, they don't have the time to "be" what Christ wants them to be. They tend to be more like Martha than Mary.

> **"Fervent prayer by at least a few people is necessary for a revival to start."**

Martha was so busy working for Christ that she missed out on the intimate times of fellowship and teaching that came from the presence of Christ. (John 12:1-11).

■ *Take for granted the grace of God* Just as married couples can begin to take one another for granted, so Christians can become so familiar with the grace of God that they lose sight of its significance. His marvelous grace, the divine nature of which we can partake and our eternal home can all become terms we speak about but fail to comprehend or appreciate.

Isaiah talks about the need for personal and corporate revival and the promise of God in providing it for His children. If Isaiah 57:14-21 were followed, not only would individuals experience renewal but so would churches, cities and nations. We need to remove the obstacles to revival, renew the promise of revival and then we will receive the results of revival.

Remove The Obstacles To Revival

"And it will be said: 'Build up, build up, prepare the road! Remove the obstacles out of the way of my people.'" (Isaiah 57:14)

Interstate 69 going west from my home in Port Huron, Michigan, was built where no road previously existed. It was interesting to look across the vacant land and see this wide stretch of excavated dirt turn into a modern four lane highway. The low areas had to be filled in and the high places lowered to give the kind of road bed needed to handle the anticipated traffic. For many who had traveled down the old two lane death trap highway, this new road couldn't get finished too soon.

The old road consisted of too few places to pass, too many

deadly crossings, and little space for relaxed driving. I would often dream what it would be like to drive this new stretch of highway with the car set on cruise control, not needing to continually anticipate the next pass, or fearful someone would be crossing left of center or failing to stop at one of the many intersections.

The day finally arrived when the road was finished. What a joy and delight. I was not disappointed. However, a tremendous amount of work and money had gone into getting the road ready for traffic. From the original planner, to the engineers, to the excavator, to the men who laid the concrete, and finally to the people who did the final work of putting up the signs and striping, the roadway took many months and years. At long last, traffic effortlessly traveled this stretch of road.

There is also much work in preparing for a revival. The need for prayer and repentance by the church, the concern for the lost and the preparing of the soil of the heart to receive not only the Word of God but also the Spirit of God, are critical.

Dr. R.A. Torrey gave the following prescription for revival:

"I can give a prescription that will bring a revival to any church or community or any city on earth.

1. Let a few Christians (they need not be many) get thoroughly right with God themselves. This is the prime essential. If this is not done, the rest that I am to say will come to nothing.

2. Let them bind themselves together in a prayer group to pray for a revival until God opens the heavens and comes down.

3. Let them put themselves at the disposal of God for Him to use as He sees fit in winning others to Christ. That is all!

This is sure to bring a revival to any church or community. I have given this prescription around the world. It has been taken by many churches and many communities, and in no instance has it ever failed; and it cannot fail!"

Let's restate those basic principles:

Prayer

Someone has said that "prayer is not the preparation for the work: it is the work." Several years ago I was going through one of the dry times in my personal life when habit and routine were carrying me, but it was not what I wanted. I didn't have the fresh sense of the anointing of the Lord. I prayed, but not with fervor, anticipation or excitement.

While on a trip to a retreat, I listened to a tape on prayer. It challenged me and was welcome food for my soul. I determined that with the help of the Lord I would rise earlier than I had been doing and devote myself to extended times of prayer. Prayer would become a priority with me.

I look back on this occasion with great fondness. It was a significant turning point in my ministry. It became the source of power for what had become a weakened personal ministry.

Also, it was this close communion with God that carried me through the frustrations of leading the local opposition against a proposed casino coming to our city. Prayer made the difference. I found a new communion with God that had been missing too long. I discovered that I "expected" God to answer prayer. It was truly exciting. Fervent prayer by at least a few people is necessary for a revival to start.

If one negative thing would characterize the American Christian church in general, it would be that it is prayerless.

Personal Preparation

"Break up your unplowed ground; for it is time to seek the LORD, until he comes and showers righteousness on you." (Hosea 10:12)

The unplowed ground represents the spiritual soil of the heart that has laid fallow for too long. It is not ready to receive the Word of God. It must now be reworked. Human effort is needed to correct this situation. The great prescription for revival given in Solomon's prayer in 2 Chronicles 7:14 talks about what the people of God are to do. They are to "Humble themselves and pray and seek my face and turn from their wicked ways." This involves personal preparation, yielding to the will of God, praying and looking to God.

Revival can hit people like a bolt of lighting, but more usually it comes after a time of preparation. Praying and heeding the Word of God make the soil ready for the Holy Spirit to come and bring the refreshing that is so badly needed.

The prophet Elijah prepared for battle with the prophets of Baal and challenged the people of Israel to recommit themselves to the living God. What Elijah saw as the first item of business is interesting. In 1 Kings 18:30 he discovers the need to repair the broken altar of God. This was something he needed to do and could do. In comparison, that is the same for an individual. They also can repair the broken altar in their lives. They can restore the broken pieces of a devotional life that has become withered. They can clean up the debris of a mouth that has become critical or a spirit that has become calloused. **Repairing the altars of our lives is part of our responsibility of getting ready for revival.**

Just prior to the opening of that new highway, the barriers were removed from the "on" ramps so the traffic could flow freely. In a similar sense, barriers need to be removed from our lives before revival can come. Pride, false hopes of salvation, rebellion, critical spirit and lack of love are just a few of the barriers that need to come down.

Renewing The Promise Of Revival

"For this is what the high and lofty One says—he who lives forever, whose name is holy: 'I live in a high and holy place, but also with him who is contrite and lowly in spirit, to revive the spirit of the lowly and to revive the heart of the contrite.'" (Isaiah 57:15)

The Author of Revival

■ *Divine Recognition* "High and lofty One says... 'I live in a high and holy place.'" Here is the Highest and Holiest talking on the subject of revival. He is preparing to tell us the secret of spiritual success by introducing us to the One who can give it. He wants us to enjoy it more than anyone else.

Revelation 21 and 22 give us a glimpse of the eternal home of the redeemed and describes the nature of the place where we will spend eternity. It is particularly noted for the absence of anything evil. It is a holy place. Revelation 21:4 reminds us that "there will be no more death or mourning or crying or pain, for the old order of things has passed away." Chapter 22:15 says, "outside are the dogs, those who practice magic arts, the sexually immoral, the murderers, the idolaters and everyone who loves and practices falsehood."

Not only is heaven holy, but it is also the dwelling place of the High and Lofty One. It is the place where God dwells. His very nature requires that we also be holy. The fires of revival flow from the heart and nature of God into the hearts of the humble and contrite.

■ *Divine Credentials* "He who lives forever, whose name is holy..." He is eternal and holy. The one who can revive the wounded heart and the thirsty soul is the one who Himself does not need to be refreshed and never grows tired or weary.

Furthermore, the Holy One calls us to be like Him and is also able to do it.

The Source Of Revival

"I live in a high and holy place, but also with him who is contrite and lowly in spirit, to revive the spirit of the lowly and to revive the heart of the contrite." (Isaiah 57:15).

■ *God lives with the contrite and lowly in spirit.* In Matthew 5:3-10 we have the words of Jesus that relate to the promise for the poor and lowly in spirit. He is talking about those who come to Christ with no preconceived ideas of their own worth. They recognize what the Apostle Paul understood about himself: that "nothing good lives in me, that is, in my sinful nature" (Romans

7:18). It is to such a one that God makes Himself available. The door of their heart is open for Christ to enter.

There are many other verses that share the wonderful hope of revival for the sincere and seeking heart.

> "The LORD is close to the brokenhearted and saves those who are crushed in spirit." (Psalms 34:18)

> "The sacrifices of God are a broken spirit; a broken and contrite heart, O God, you will not despise." (Psalms 51:17)

> "Has not my hand made all these things, and so they came into being?" declares the LORD. "This is the one I esteem: he who is humble and contrite in spirit, and trembles at my word." (Isaiah 66:2)

> "They have chosen their own ways, and their soul delights in their abominations;... for when I called, no one answered, when I spoke, no one listened. They did evil in my sight and chose what displeases me." (Isaiah 66:3b,4b)

> "Rend your heart and not your garments. Return to the LORD your God, for he is gracious and compassionate, slow to anger and abounding in love, and he relents from sending calamity." (Joel 2:13)

> "Godly sorrow brings repentance that leads to salvation and leaves no regret, but worldly sorrow brings death." (2 Corinthians 7:10)

"Contrite" means to be penitent and remorseful. It means turning away from sin. Until one is ready to do this, the hand and presence of God will be hindered from coming.

Picture that the high, lofty and holy God, who dwells outside His creation, is also willing and able to live with His created provided they are lowly and humble of heart.

Being contrite and lowly has nothing to do with the socioeconomic status of a person. It has everything to do with the attitude of the heart. I have known wealthy and poor who are very humble and wealthy and poor who are very proud.

The secret of revival is to have the Holy God of the Universe dwelling and reigning in the life of each person.

You may have pitted yourself against Almighty God—wanting to go your own way. You have refused to bend your neck and surrender your will to the will of God. You have resisted salvation through Christ and have insisted that your road to heaven is as valid as Christ's. If that is indeed your attitude then you will find yourself to be fighting against God and you will be the loser.

My friend, bend your neck, bow your knee, confess the name of Jesus. Then you will sense the freedom and joy you have only dreamed of up to this point.

Receiving The Results Of Revival

"...to revive the spirit of the lowly and to revive the heart of the contrite." (Isaiah 57:15)

"I will not accuse forever, nor will I always be angry, for then the spirit of man would grow faint before me—the breath of man that I have created." (Isaiah 57:16)

"I have seen his ways, but I will heal him; I will guide him and restore comfort to him." (Isaiah 57:18)

"Creating praise on the lips of the mourners in Israel. 'Peace, peace, to those far and near,' says the LORD. "And I will heal them." (Isaiah 57:19)

Notice the action in the above verses that is promised for the contrite in heart. God will revive the spirit, not accuse him forever... heal him, guide him, restore comfort to him, create praise on his lips and give him peace. God offers a revival of spirit. What a promise!

You may be thinking this is just what the nonbeliever needs to hear, however it is primarily intended for those who have professed faith in Jesus Christ, but have cooled off and gotten careless.

My heart trembles inside me when I think of those in congregations around the world who attend Sunday morning services, but have little commitment to God or His church.

We need spiritual giants to lead the way for the new babes in Christ. We can't depend on those who have gone to be with the Lord. We have moved into their spots. Many of you are now the age of those you remember as your spiritual mentors. The ones I am talking to are making the memories for our young people and young adults.

Some of you need to seek God's face in earnest or the day of revival will pass you by. His Spirit will not always strive with you. He may have been wooing you for some time but if in your pride and stubbornness you continue to resist, He may just put you on a spiritual shelf where you can't do any harm. Paul was concerned that after he had preached he would become a castaway, part of the dried up branches.

What are the steps to bring revival to the serious hearted? What should you do if you long for a life-changing spirit of renewal? What are the keys to see that it happens?

1. Remember "the height from which you have fallen" (Revelation 2:5). If you have left your first love, remember how you felt at the beginning? Do you feel that way now? How far have you slipped? How have you changed?

2. Repent (Revelation 2:5). There is no long lasting cure without repentance. You need to ask God to forgive you for wandering away from His love. Has your heart grown cold even though you still go through the motions? Do you have a censorious spirit that has badly wounded the church? You need to repent. Is the Holy Spirit impressing upon you the need to repent of some hidden sin? Then you need to repent of it.

3. Do "the things you did at first" (Revelation 2:5). Christian, what did you do after you were first converted? Do you remember when the coals for God were burning hot in your heart? You probably devoured the Word, regularly attended church, witnessed to friends, practiced personal purity, loved to pray. **DO ALL THOSE THINGS AGAIN.**

Do you have great seasons of prayer when the flood gates of glory seem to open up? Are you regularly discovering new nuggets of truth from God's Word that help you in your Christian growth? Do some of the individuals on your prayer list get converted? Do you practice sacrificial giving? Do you rejoice with what God is doing in His world? Are your times of devotions still precious and rewarding? Do you weep over the erring and the lost?

If not many of your answers to the above questions were in the affirmative, then it is time for a revival of your spirit. Psalms 51:17 says, "The sacrifices of God are a broken spirit; a broken and contrite heart, O God, you will not despise."

But, how does one get a "broken and contrite spirit?" This condition of the spirit can only come out of an intense desire for God to restore you to a place of spiritual victory. Repent and turn from sin and God will graciously meet your need. God promises revival for those who will seek it with their whole heart.

8

CHAPTER

Quit Whining, Try Mining

"Trust in the Lord and do good;
dwell in the land and enjoy safe pasture.
Delight yourself in the Lord and
He will give you the desires of your heart."
(Psalms 37:3-5)

More than one-half of Jesus' parables deal with the subject of material possessions. This was a familiar topic to our Lord. Jesus knew how important this subject was to people, so He addressed it often.

At an early age we learn something about money: earning, spending and saving. What parent hasn't been pestered by a small child wanting to set up a street-side lemonade stand or hoping to win that wonderful prize if they can only sell 150 candy bars? They may also soon learn that they can earn some needed money by helping around the house.

There is nothing wrong with material resources or the accumulation of material resources. In fact, the Bible talks about the needs we have and how we are to work to provide for those needs. It even encourages savings and prosperity. What the Bible warns about is the "love of money": that strong desire for wealth and possessions that gets our focus off what is really important. This chapter is not a complete teaching on the idea of Christian stewardship but rather focuses on God's promises as they relate to our resources. **I want to focus on three main areas that relate to resources: our attitude, our acquisition, and our usage.**

Our Attitude

■ *We must recognize God's ownership.* Everything belongs to God. Man thinks he owns this piece of land or that building or those cattle, but they are all God's and only leased back to man for a specific period of time.

"The earth is the Lord's and everything in it." (Psalms 24:1)

"For every animal in the forest is mine, and the cattle on a thousand hills." (Psalms 50:10)

"The silver is mine and the gold is mine, declares the Lord Almighty." (Haggai 2:8)

"What do you have that you did not receive?" (1 Corinthians 4:7)

■ *Resources are uncertain.* We may have great wealth today, but it can be lost in a matter of days or less. On October 19, 1987, the Dow Jones' industrial average dropped over 500 points. This was the largest one-day drop in the New York Stock Exchange history. Amounts lost that day by individuals were $3.1 billion, $1.9 billion, $845 million, $1.5 billion, $991 million, $829 million, $502 million, $883 million and $272 million. While most of this money was only represented on paper, it was still a tremendous loss of wealth in one eight-hour period. Earthly wealth has no guarantee.

Jesus warned of the avarice that causes one to be constantly concerned about storing up treasures on earth where wealth can be corroded or stolen while, on the other hand, not getting rich in Heaven (Matthew 6:20). Paul cautioned rich Christians not to "put their hope in wealth, which is so uncertain (1 Timothy 6:17). I heard Dr. Ben Lew tell how in concentration camps in Germany during the Second World War costly items of jewelry such as diamond rings, necklaces, etc. meant nothing. These items could lay on the floor for days and no one would bother to pick them up. What good is costly apparel when you are starving to death or ready to face the gas chamber?

Our Acquisitions

■ *All our needs will be supplied.* These are the words of Jesus reassuring a fearful people that every basic need would be supplied by a loving Father.

> "And my God will meet all your needs..." (Philippians 4:19)

> "And do not set your heart on what you will eat or drink; do not worry about it. For the pagan world runs after such things, and your Father knows that you need them. But seek his kingdom, and these things will be given to you as well." (Luke 12:29-31)

> "But seek first his kingdom and his righteousness, and all these things will be given to you as well." (Matthew 6:33)

Two thoughts come out of these last verses that have been a tremendous source of help to me; God knows what we need and God meets our need.

Each summer my wife, without apology, begins to ask God for school clothes for the children for the coming school year. That is a need God knows we have.

The Father knows we need places of refuge, food to eat, and clothes to wear.

One year we planned on moving to make it financially easier for our children to receive a college education. We put our house up for sale and started looking for one with lower payments. We had no trouble going to God and asking Him to lead us to the right one. We were His children; and He knew our needs. I can't say we never grew anxious, but it was comforting to know that God was interested and would get personally involved in our situation. He was going to help us find the right home. Jesus had said that our Father "knows what we need."

Jesus had no doubt that the God who knew our needs would also meet our needs. He didn't want us to waste precious time and energy worrying about such things. He demonstrates the folly of such worry by asking "who can add an hour to his life worrying about it?" (Matthew 6:27) He also demonstrates how beautifully God cares for the birds and the flowers of the field. Jesus sums up this passage by stating, "If that is how God clothes the grass of the field, will he not much more clothe you..." (Matthew 6:30). Now, back to my wife's prayers for our clothes.

Each new season of the year, especially before school begins, Margaret assesses the needs of each family member and then asks God to supply the particular items. The Lord has always provided for those needs through hand-me-downs, garage sales, or special sales. Several times someone has been impressed to either take a family member shopping or to give us a gift certificate to a clothing store. There have been times when she asked for a certain color "if it would please the Lord" and He has answered specifically.

When our daughter was a junior in high school, she was going on a band trip to Florida. Because of a new growth spurt, she had outgrown her summer clothes and needed several outfits. My wife was planning to do some sewing for Jackie but it was a very busy time for her. She and Jackie together asked the Lord to provide some cotton clothes. Several hours later, a lady in our congregation called and said she felt God impressing her to call and see if we had any specific needs. She especially wondered about Jackie. My wife hesitated at first to make the clothing needs known but then remembered this could be the Lord answering prayer. After hearing about the needs, the lady gave Jackie a J.C. Penney gift certificate.

Another time my wife and I were getting ready to attend our Denominational Conference where I would be on the platform a considerable amount of time. My wife felt both the responsibility and the concern for seeing that our clothes were ready for the trip. At that time, our wardrobes consisted mainly of old and worn items. Therefore, Margaret again asked the Lord to supply the clothes we would need for this Conference and the season to follow. Well, the Lord answered more abundantly than we were

> **"I like to think that God beams with joy when He has the opportunity to respond to our faith."**

able to ask or even imagine. We were both given some beautiful new outfits and accessories. We had never felt so finely attired from head to foot. Someone had been willing to be used by God to meet our need. God had given us far more than we had ever imagined.

What about the houses we had to sell and buy? Margaret and I were coming home from one of our boy's soccer games on a Monday evening and were talking about how we would go about selling the house. We had put it on the market several years earlier, but not one person went through it. As we discussed the matter, we decided to list it with a real estate agent the next day. When we arrived home, there was a car in the driveway and a man at our front door. We inquired as to what he wanted. He was looking for a vacant lot like the one beside us or for a four bedroom home with a basement. We didn't have a vacant lot but we did have the house. He asked if he and the interested family could come in and see the house right then (9:30 at night!). He gave us a few minutes to throw a few things under the bed and then they toured our house that was not yet on the market. They came back the next morning to see it again, and by Thursday of the same week the deal was closed. What seems to make this more amazing to us was that there were homes on both sides of us that had For Sale signs on them. The buyer had no idea we were interested in selling, but God did and He knew the timing was right. We believe He put them there at that time for us.

We now had thirty days to find another place and move. My wife and her father spent days looking for a place for us. About the time we would make an offer the salesman would call and say it had just been sold. The days were fast approaching when we would have to be out of the house. Where would we store all the things a family of six had accumulated? Where would we live?

Three things we were looking for in a house were: 1) a large place for our boys to play outside, 2) a study for me and 3) a house with payments that would fit our budget.

Just days before we had to move, one of our staff wives called and said a house just down from them was for sale. We made contact immediately with the salesperson to go through the house. It had a very small backyard, but bordered an elementary school yard. This provided several acres of yard for the boys, which we didn't have to mow or pay for. It also had a nice little study nook for me and payments we could afford.

But what about getting in on time? We were just a week away from when we needed to be out of the other house. The Lord knew about that, too. It was convenient for the lady who owned the house to move her things out so we could move right in. We didn't have to store a thing or spend a night at anyone else's house. Our Father took care of all the details.

There are some very beautiful stories about God's concern for our basic needs from 1 & 2 Kings.

Elijah is fed by ravens. (1 Kings 17:1-6)

The supply of oil and flour that never ran out.(1 Kings 17:7-24)

The widow and the jars of oil. (2 Kings 4:1-7)

Feeding 100 prophets with just 20 loaves of bread. (2 Kings 4:42-44)

The axe head floats. (2 Kings 6:1-7)

God routs the army and the siege is lifted. (2 Kings 7:3-20)

The passage in 2 Kings 4:1-7 has a special meaning to me. It was in late February a few years ago and the church budget was running a $7500.00 deficit after only two months. January and February are usually difficult months for cash flow in the church but this year seemed worse than before. I mentioned the need in the weekly church paper and asked the congregation to pray about it. I figured that people would have to dig a little deeper and we would care for the need over the next several months. I went about my normal pastoral duties and didn't give a great deal of thought to it other than God would have to help us.

On Thursday of that week I spoke for a senior citizens gathering at another church on the subject of the widow's oil. My text was taken from 2 Kings 4. I remember stressing to the group of seniors that God didn't specify how many empty vessels the widow was to gather, but that she was to get a lot of them, as many as she could. Then, she was to start pouring the little oil she did have into the jars she had collected. As she started to pour that little bit of oil, God miraculously kept making oil until every vessel was full. Then and only then did the source of oil stop. I challenged the seniors to believe God for their every need in spite of their meager earnings or savings. I reminded them that faith helps us to gather more vessels because it was no more a miracle to fill the last jar than the first one. God could have filled two hundred as easily as He could two.

I went back to my office to continue my work. My secretary came in and said that a lady and her daughter from our congregation were there to see me. I knew the lady was a widow and I had talked with both of them some at the door on Sundays, but I didn't know them well. We chatted for a few minutes and then she stated the purpose of her visit.

She had recently made a settlement with the insurance company relating to the death of her husband and had money she wanted to tithe. She and her daughter had been praying about where to give the money when they saw our church's need. She felt led to give it to our church. She wanted to give it where she was worshipping. The amount of the check was exactly the amount of our deficit. Did that just happen by chance? I don't think so. God knew our needs and what we were attempting to do to reach our world for Him. He saw the "vessels" we had been gathering in which to receive the oil of His faithfulness. He supplied the need. It seemed impossible to me to have the need met in a minute, but not so with God. It was no more a miracle for Him to bring it all at once than over several months. If you have put God first and sought His kingdom above everything else, you have every right to gather vessels by faith and ask God to fill them and to depend upon God to meet your needs. God delights in doing it.

I like to think that God beams with joy when He has the opportunity to respond to our faith. He has promised so much, but lack of faith stymies the fulfillment.

A new resident of Heaven was being shown around by one of the angels. They were looking in the various rooms at all the lovely places. They came to one door that the angel seemed hesitant to open. The new resident inquired about the contents of the room and why the angel hesitated to open it. After much urging, the door was opened and inside were hundreds of beautiful packages. "What are all of these gifts?" the new resident asked. "These are all the good things God promised to give you while on earth if you would only have asked and believed," said the angel.

The future is as bright as God's promises to meet all our needs, yet we often go around in poverty of spirit because we fail to ask.

■ *We need to be committed to the Lord.* When Moses was instructed to choose men to help him govern Israel, one of the requirements was that they were to be "trustworthy men who hate dishonest gain" (Exodus 18:21).

God is not running some gigantic world welfare system. There are certain things that God requires on our part to activate His generosity to us. God loves to care for His own family more than you or I want to care for ours. However, just as we teach responsibility to our children and give them little things to do to help them feel they have earned something, God does something similar. There is no way our small children can ever earn everything we give them. They just don't have the resources. In the same way, we could never do enough to repay God for every gift given to us. But what does He require? What does He ask of us?

"Trust in the Lord and do good; dwell in the land and enjoy safe pasture. Delight yourself in the Lord and he will give you the desires of your heart. Commit your way to the Lord; trust in him and he will do this." (Psalms 37:3-5)

"There are certain things that God requires on our part to activate his generosity to us."

This verse is packed with promises including safety, food, relaxation, and a dream book, but notice the requirements: 1) trust in the Lord, 2) do good, 3) delight in the Lord, and 4) commit your way to the Lord. Nowhere does it talk about being able to pay God back for all the things given; He doesn't ask for that. He only wants us to trust and serve Him.

There is an interesting comparison between Psalms 37:4 and Psalms 106:15. The verses in Psalms 37:3-5 carry the thought of everything good. You just get the feeling that whatever God gives you will be beautiful, pleasing and more than enough. To receive all this, He only asks us to delight in Him and trust Him. In Psalms 106:15 God also gave the people of Israel what they wanted. They asked for meat to eat because they were not satisfied with the manna God was providing. God gave it to them in abundance. However, in so doing, He also gave them a "wasting disease" or a plague that consumed many of them. What made the difference? Why was one verse so pleasant and the other so horrible? They both asked and they both received what they wanted. The key is found in the desire of the one doing the asking. Psalms 37:4 starts with a heart devoted to God while in 106:15 the person starts with their own desires with little thought of God. When we set our heart on God, He changes our wants to bring them into conformity with His will. When we delight in the Lord first, our desires will be such that God will delight to honor them. He'll love it.

This verse became real to me when I was a sophomore in college. I was working in a small factory in Walled Lake, Michigan, and also assisting in a small church during the summer months. My real love was the church work, but I needed a full time job so I

> "When we set our heart on God, He changes our wants to bring them into conformity with His will."

could make some money to go back to college in the fall. My job was not the most exciting in the world, but it did provide me with some needed money. The plant where I worked made water tanks for small travel trailers and my job was to do both low pressure tests and high pressure tests for leaks in the welds. One day the boss came to me and began to talk about driving the semi-truck and doing deliveries. That to me was an exciting possibility. You have to know that I had always wanted to drive such a truck not only around town and across the state but from coast to coast. I know that doesn't sound too much like the goals of one who had his heart set on the ministry since he was 12, but that was a dream I had. The next day the boss came and took me on a trial run. We went around a four mile square. My driving must have satisfied him for he told me to get my lunch and take the load to Elkhart, Indiana, a trip of some 200 miles. What a delight. I was getting to partially fulfill my dream.

All that summer I drove throughout the Midwest delivering water tanks to various trailer factories. Then one day the boss came and said he had another job he wanted me to do. He was moving his plant to Hemet, California, and wanted me, along with another fellow in the shop to take a truck load of equipment to the new plant. I remember going to the home of the pastoral family I was staying with and telling them about the upcoming trip and how that had always been my dream. The pastor then shared with me the verse which says if we delight in the Lord then He delights to give us the desires of our hearts.

After reaching our destination in California and driving the few miles to the coast, I remember thinking how completely God gives us our desires when we delight in Him. Who would have thought that a 19-year-old ministerial student would ever have had the opportunity to have such a dream fulfilled, but God delighted to do it. I think He jumped with glee and had a great big smile on His face when He saw how He had delighted me. He put me in the right place at the right time so it could come to pass. What a promise!

Friend, delight first in the Lord. Seek His kingdom and His righteousness and the other things you need and even the desires of your heart will be fulfilled.

■ *Diligence brings rewards.* God delights in doing for us what we cannot do for ourselves, but He doesn't necessarily do for us what we can do for ourselves. The book of Proverbs particularly speaks to the promises of our diligence. Proverbs 10:4 says, "...diligent hands bring wealth" and 12:24 adds, "Diligent hands will rule, but laziness ends in slave labor." Proverbs 26:13-15 describes the man who is lazy and refuses to work. Should this person expect God to take care of them? The author seems to think not. He says, "The sluggard says, `There is a lion in the road, a fierce lion roaming the streets! As a door turns on its hinges, so a sluggard turns on his bed. The sluggard buries his hand in the dish; he is too lazy to bring it back to his mouth.'" There is little help or hope for the lazy person. Paul told those at Thessalonica who quit working because they thought the second coming was near, that if they didn't work they shouldn't expect someone to give them a handout. He makes it even stronger in 1 Timothy 5:8: "If anyone does not provide for his relatives, and especially for his immediate family, he has denied the faith and is worse than an unbeliever." Remember, this is the same fellow that said "God will supply all your needs." Our willingness to do what we can and be as wise as we can makes the difference. God knows our hearts and our efforts and lovingly will make up the difference.

One Winter, we had a rather heavy snow of about 8-10 inches. The schools were called off and so our boys were home. I challenged our 12-year-old to get out and clean some sidewalks and I even volunteered the snow blower if he wanted to use it. He took me up on the offer. Early in the morning, he and his nine-year-old brother started down the street on their business venture. The snow plows had not yet plowed the side streets so it was with great effort that they trudged through the heavy snow. On my way to work I followed their path and saw the one brother cleaning a path with the snow shovel so the other brother could pull the snow blower. After several hours, they came home with the discouraging news that no one wanted their sidewalks cleaned. All that walking and pulling with no response.

If I had known that business would have been so bad after they had worked so hard, I would have paid someone to let the boys do their walks. I wanted them to have some success. I wanted to see some sense of satisfaction on their countenance.

I think God responds in a similar manner. We may work hard, make some bad decisions, and not always use our money wisely, but God sees how hard we have tried and still comes to our rescue. He supplies our needs.

The Usage Of Our Resources

It is in this area that we find additional promises for the believer.

■ *Needs Of The Family* "So do not worry, saying, `What shall we eat' or `What shall we drink?' or 'What shall we wear?' For the pagans run after all these things, and **Your heavenly father knows what you need**." (Matthew 6:31-32).

■ *Planning For The Future* In Luke 12 there is the story of the rich farmer. God does not condemn the man because he planned ahead or that he possessed great wealth, but that he forgot God. This man did not even consider God. He thought everything was for himself and that his ingenuity and hard work had gotten him everything. The Bible commends those who plan ahead and remember God in the process.

■ *Helping In The Lord's Work* "Honor the Lord with your wealth, with the first fruits of all your crops; then your barns will be filled to overflowing, and your vats will brim over with new wine" (Proverbs 3:9-10). What a promise! Fantastic!

The Request: "Honor the Lord with your wealth and the first fruits." The first fruits were the first crops taken off. This was an indication that God deserved the first and the best. The first of everything belongs to God. Too often we wait until the end and then give God what is left. In most households, if we gave God what was left after we finished paying all the bills, there would be nothing to give Him. I believe that's why God wants us to bring the first fruits. A method I have used in teaching tithing to my congregation is the little phrase, "Tithe off the top and bills off the bottom." The tithe comes out first. That is like the first fruit.

The Promise: "Your barns will be filled" and "Your vats will run over." What a joy to give knowing that God will honor your giving. We don't give to get, but we do have the promise that when we give God will see that we are cared for.

Too many Christians have not yet learned the joy of such a walk. They still have either not committed themselves to the work of God or they haven't learned to trust God for their needs. They haven't discovered they cannot out give God.

Psalms 37:26 describes those who give freely to others yet still have all they need. It seems like a paradox, but it is a promise. I have often marveled at how God could make the nine-tenths that remained go as far, if not farther, than the ten-tenths when I tried keeping it for myself. When the Children of Israel were in the wilderness, God reminded them that their shoes or clothes did not wear out and He always provided the manna and meat. Brian Ake, our former music director, used to sing a song about giving our possessions out the front door and God shoveling more in the back door. How true that is.

When we give God what is His, we discover his promises work in everyday life. One of the greatest thrills of my life has been observing God supply our needs. When you tithe in obedience to God's Word, you have every right to ask and expect Him to help you meet your obligations. You will prove Him to be true to His Word. We are not to put God to a foolish test by expecting Him to protect us if we jump off the top of a building but we are told to "prove" Him when it comes to financial matters.

I remember one time when I was sinfully burdened with fear over a certain financial matter. It troubled me night and day and I couldn't concentrate on my work.

During that period of time I was serving as an evangelist at a camp, but because of my preoccupation with financial matters, I did not feel spiritually well prepared to minister. While praying about the matter, I sensed the Lord saying to me, as if He had been sitting on the chair across from me, "You quit worrying about those bills. I will take care of you." I can't explain the peace that came to my heart after that encounter. It was nothing short of a miracle. I'm not saying I never felt a twinge of worry after that, but the consuming fear that had gripped me was gone **and God proved Himself faithful.**

We Are To Give God The Tithe

The average evangelical church only receives approximately 5% of the available tithe. When you stop to think that some people will give more than 10%, you then realize that a lot of people are giving less than 5% to the Lord. How can they expect the blessing of God? How can they live in disobedience and expect to know His fullness?

I once was doing a study of the giving of one of my congregations. I was a young pastor and assuming that everyone was tithing. However, I began to go down the list of regular attenders and conservatively estimated their salaries. It was not a scientific study, but I made sure I was realistic in my "guestimations." It was a startling revelation to me when I finished my project. I couldn't believe it. There were professing Christians that were not giving to God the tithe of their income. I remember falling on my knees and confessing to God that we didn't have a money problem, but a sin problem. How could we expect the blessing of God when we were robbing God of what was His?

"Robbing God" is not the cloak and dagger crime that is portrayed on television, but it is a white collar crime where we simply defraud God of what is His. In other words, what are we buying with money that belongs to God?

Malachi 3 gives us the clearest teaching and promise on the subject of the tithe.

The Request: "Bring the whole tithe into the storehouse." There is wide consent that the storehouse today is the local church. This is the place for the tithe.

The Result: "That there may be food in my house."

There are some wonderful things that happen when God's people give to Him what he has asked them to give. The Lord's work will not lack resources.

It is a tragic state of affairs in the Christian church when the work of God goes undernourished because those who call themselves Christians are not giving God His tithe. The low salaries some pastors receive is almost criminal, considering scriptures say they are worthy of "double-honor." Christian missions struggle to pay basic bills let alone put the badly needed missionaries on the field and pay them a living wage. The lack of missionary candidates may well be tied to the lack of tithing support by the people of God. Christian colleges are fighting for survival financially. Many of these are excellent schools with an impressive list of alumni who are making a significant contribution to the Christian world.

God thought out His plan well in advance before giving it to Abraham after his rescue of Lot. God knew the tithe would be more than adequate to meet the demands of His work. There would be enough food in his house so all could be cared for. When the church struggles because of insufficient funds, it is probably because some are not giving the tithe.

One of the great joys of giving is that I can be a participant in God's work. By bringing my tithe into the storehouse, I help His work go forward. I get a thrill out of seeing lives changed, marriages restored, and people having hope of eternal life.

Several years ago I attended a chapel at Bethel College in Mishawaka, Indiana. A young Indian girl provided the special music. She gave the following story: Her grandfather had been a Hindu priest and every morning he would go to the Hindu temple and make a sacrifice to various gods. But her grandfather would also cry out to an unknown God to show him more if there was more to know. Surely there must be more! About that time, a missionary arrived in the village to tell the people about Jesus. He had to cross a river that was one and one-half miles wide and filled with crocodiles to get to the village. They don't know where this missionary came from or who he was, but he brought a message of salvation and her grandfather was converted. She said, "If salvation had not come, I would still go daily to the Hindu temple, break open a coconut and sacrifice it to my god." Christian missions need meat in the Father's house. When people live in obedience to God's Word by giving their tithe, it is bound to do something for the spirit of the church. Such obedience will bring revival.

Do you feel spiritually depressed? Defeated? Lack a spiritual joy you think ought to be there? Just as you can't have any joy with your parents or your boss when you are ignoring their clear instructions, so it is with our relationship with God.

■ *God is proved true.* Some feel the blessings referred to in Malachi are spiritual, but even if they are, author R.T. Kendall points out how "God has a way of blessing us materially that just happens to coincide with our having become tithers. The 90% that we keep to ourselves after the tithe is given to the Lord has a way of equalling the 100% before the tithe. Sometimes the 90% goes far beyond what that 100% would have purchased." How can this be? I personally don't know, but I believe it!

■ *God will open the windows of Heaven.* If we apply these verses only to material gain we may well miss the spiritual application God had in mind, but I don't think we can ignore the fact that God intends to bless us materially.

Reward is not the main reason for tithing, but God certainly does not rule out rewards. "Who among us can do anything indefinitely without some kind of encouragement from God? Who can pray daily and faithfully for many days without there being some token of God's smile? All of us need encouragement. God knows this. "O taste and see that the Lord is good" (Psalms 34:8). "I will sing unto the Lord, because he hath dealt bountifully with me" (Psalms 13:6). "Bless the Lord, o my soul, and forget not all his benefits" (Psalms 103:2). "Even though God would not have to promise a blessing if we obey, He always does...**God never demands obedience without a promise of blessing.**"

> **"When people live in obedience to God's Word by giving their tithe, it is bound to do something for the spirit of the Church."**

A successful business man was asked the key to his success: "The answer to that is very simple. Many years ago I made a contract with the Lord, claiming the promise: 'Them that honor me I will honor' (1 Samuel 2:30). I began tithing." He went on to say he began tithing when he had almost no income, even when he could not 'afford' to tithe. He kept his contract with the Lord. God began blessing him as he went from one level of business to another."

J. Wilbur Chapman recounted the story about a woman from his congregation who shared with the church how she felt God had failed in providing her material needs in spite of her faithfulness in tithing. She explained that she was soon retiring, but had no money saved and the company she worked for had no pension plan for its employees. She lamented, "For many years I have given to the Lord's cause; now, when I am old and not able to work, I face direst poverty.... I must tell God that He has not cared for me as He promised."

Shortly after the woman's testimony, Mr. Chapman was invited out to lunch by the owner of the company where the woman was employed. The businessman excitedly shared how the company was instituting a pension plan for employees and that a member of Pastor Chapman's church was to be the first beneficiary. The woman who had complained just a little while earlier was to be the first employee to get retirement benefits from the company. God was faithful as He promised.

W.A. Criswell told about the pastor who was asked, "How many church members do you have?"

The answer was, "One hundred fifty."

The pastor was further asked, "How many of them are tithers?"

"One hundred fifty," he responded.

In astonishment the inquirer exclaimed, "What! All one hundred fifty, the entire church, are tithers?"

"Yes indeed," said the pastor. "About fifty of them bring the tithe to the storehouse, and God collects it from the rest."

We can bring our tithe as an act of worship or we can let God extract it from us by other means and miss the blessing of giving joyfully to Him. God has many promises that relate to our resources but much of it is tied to our giving of the tithe.

Friend, are you burdened with worry because of the financial concerns in your life? If you have honored God with what is His and sought His kingdom above everything else, you have every right to go to Him and ask for His help. Leave your burden with Him and watch how He will miraculously meet your need.

9
CHAPTER

I Didn't Know That!

*"Do not suppose that I have come to bring peace to the earth.
I did not come to bring peace, but a sword."*
(Matthew 10:34)

Jesus expected a commitment from His disciples that was costly. When Jesus commissioned his twelve, He did not paint a very rosy picture for them. Jesus was straightforward in advising them what it would cost to be one of His followers. He did not require tremendous intellect though I think the disciples were intelligent men. He did, however, expect their loyalty and commitment.

Robert Coleman in his book, *The Master Plan of Evangelism*, writes, "the disciples were not handshaking emissaries maintaining the status quo. They had a revolutionary message and they were engaged in a warfare... It soon became apparent that being a disciple of Christ involved far more than the joyful acceptance of the Messianic promise, Whoopee, he's come. It meant the surrender of one's whole life to the Master in absolute submission to His sovereignty."

While we ideally see the Christ of the manger as the Prince of Peace, there is also the awful condition of the human heart that brought the Pharisees and Jesus into sharp contention. Why would anyone oppose the man of humble birth that went around healing the lame, causing the blind to see, casting out demons, making the deaf to hear and much more? Yet, this was the one they nailed to the Cross. And Jesus let His disciples know that if this was done to Him, they could also expect the same treatment. **That is a promise.** It is not the kind of promise we go looking for, but it is nevertheless true.

Jesus Expects His Disciples To Make Difficult Commitments

Life for the disciples was not always going to be easy. Turbulent times loomed in the future for them. They were going to be persecuted in ways they had not dreamed of because of their allegiance to Jesus Christ. Jesus didn't want them to be surprised by such activity. He wanted them to know that making a commitment to Him would be very costly. Jesus gave them some of the following insights and expectations as to just how costly it would be for His disciples:

■ *Discipleship will drain you of physical and emotional energy.* "As you go, preach this message: 'The kingdom of Heaven is near. Heal the sick, raise the dead, cleanse those who have leprosy, drive out demons. Freely you have received, freely give.'" (Matthew 10:7-8). He wanted them to pour their lifeblood into people with serious needs. They would be called out early in the morning and not get home until late at night, but that is part of the commitment to following Christ.

■ *Discipleship requires freely giving of your livelihood (verses*

> "Jesus came to bring a revolution, not peaceful coexistence."

9-15). When Jesus was calling the disciples, he appeared at their various places of business and said: "Peter, I want you to follow me" and "Matthew, I want you to follow me." In every instance they got up and left their fishing nets or tax booth, followed Jesus and left it all behind. Jesus told his disciples, "When you go out on these preaching and witnessing missions to talk to people about the kingdom, I don't want you to take a big bank roll or money belt. I want you to take your bare necessities. When you enter a city, I want you to go to a home and stay there until you have finished in that area." The disciples didn't have the security of financial backing.

Jesus expects every follower to follow with his purse. There is no following without this involvement.

■ *Discipleship requires the sacrifice of your body if necessary (verses 16-20, 28-33).* Jesus said, "I am sending you out like sheep among wolves." In essence Jesus is saying, "I am not sending you out to another sheep fold. I am sending you out among wolves and you know what wolves do to sheep."

Jesus also told them they would be flogged. Now friends, I don't know whether you recognize it or not, but that was also a promise.

Not all the promises of God are for ease and comfort, rest, restoration, and renewal. I can hear Jesus saying to His followers, "I want you to understand that some of you are going to have your hands tied together, be suspended in the air and then flogged across the back at least 39 times. You will be beaten to a hair's breath of your life. I want you to understand that. That's part of the cost of being one of my disciples."

Furthermore, they are going to drag you in before kings and governors like common criminals. Jesus was even so bold to add the statement, "Do not be afraid of those who can only kill the body (verse 28)." Don't worry about those who can only take your life? Wow, what comfort! What a promise! "But rather fear the one who can destroy both body and soul in Hell." Jesus was very clear about what was to be expected. He wanted them to fear only God's displeasure and the consequences of sin that ultimately lead one to Hell.

Christian discipleship will often cause alienation in personal relationships. The community at large is not going to like you. You will be hated by all men because of Jesus (verse 22). Did you get that? The community at large won't like you because your message is a revolutionary message that goes against the status quo.

Your family may even be against you. "Brother will betray brother to death, and a father his child; children will rebel against their parents and have them put to death (verse 21)." In Matthew 10:34 Jesus goes on to say, "Do not suppose that I have come to bring peace to the earth. I did not come to bring peace, but a sword."

"Now wait a minute pastor, John 14 says, 'My peace I leave with you, not as the world gives, let not your hearts be troubled and neither let it be afraid.' Are you telling me Jesus is saying He didn't come to bring peace but a sword? What is He talking about?" John 14 speaks of inner peace that comes from a right relationship with Jesus.

Matthew 10:35-36 relates how discipleship may affect relationships within one's family. "I have come to turn a man against his father, a daughter against her mother, a mother-in-law against her daughter-in-law. A man's enemies will be the members of his own household." In essence Jesus is saying: If you are a follower of mine there may be those in your own household who won't like it and it may cause division. They may not like what you believe or give financially. Neither may they like what you do or don't do. He wants you to understand that the daughter-in-law may come to Christ and the mother-in-law not like it. Or that a son may come to Christ and the father might not like it. There may be divisions right in your own household, but I want you to understand that is part of the cost of being a disciple.

In many places in the world when a missionary leads someone to Jesus Christ, the family turns against the new believer. Some cultures even have a funeral for the person. It is as though that person no longer exists. As hard as it is to accept and as much as we don't like such promises, that is what Jesus meant. There may be alienation of relationships when we come to Jesus Christ. In Matthew 10:24 Jesus said they would persecute Him and therefore the disciples could expect similar treatment. **Jesus came to bring a revolution, not peaceful coexistence.** Peaceful coexistence was not in His vocabulary. It was not part of His plan. He never promised His disciples they could peacefully coexist with the evil around them.

Three different people came to Jesus and said they wanted to be His followers. One came and said "I will follow you wherever you go" (Matthew 8:19). In the following verse, Jesus let the man know that foxes have holes to live in and the birds have nests, but He didn't even have a place He could call His own. He wanted the man to understand what it might mean to be a disciple. Another man asked to follow Jesus, but he first wanted to be excused to care for some immediate obligations (Matthew 8:21). Jesus made it clear that the man was to come and follow right away. The third individual also expressed interest in being a disciple, but made it clear that he wanted it to be on his terms (Luke 9:61)." Jesus again stated the terms of discipleship by letting the man know that he could not follow on his terms. The man needed to be totally committed to Christ. Jesus made it clear that anyone who puts His hand on the plow, but has second thoughts and starts looking back, is not fit for the Kingdom of God (Luke 9:62)." Jesus boldly announced in Luke 14:33, "Unless you renounce all you cannot be my disciple."

Jesus Expects His Disciples
To Make Decisions That Are Revolutionary

The kind of radical discipleship that Jesus calls for demands some tough and difficult decisions. In his book *The Master Plan of Evangelism*, Robert Coleman says, "In the church at large, among the clergy and the laity, there is a general indifference to the commands of God or at least a kind of contented complacency with mediocrity. Where is the obedience of the cross? Indeed, it would appear that the teachings of Christ upon self denial, dedication, have been replaced by a sort of respectable do as you please philosophy of expediency."

Friends, the "do as you please" philosophy has not escaped churches. Many people attend church Sunday after Sunday who have nothing more than a casual acquaintance with the Savior. I'm not talking about babes in Christ. I'm talking about people who should have gone on to maturity. Christians who should have grown up in the Lord.

Several of the tough and revolutionary decisions are described for us in Matthew 10:37-39.

■ *We need to love God more than family.*

■ *We need to take up our cross daily and follow Christ.*

■ *We need to decide to lose our life here so we can find it in Christ.*

Most every serious follower of Jesus Christ has asked the question, "How much time should be devoted to my family and how much to Christian work?" There is the strong desire to put Christ first but also the sense of Christian conviction to lead our children in the faith as well. How do I devote myself fully to Christ but not lose my children in the process? I don't think this is an either/or situation. It is the balancing of priorities. Jesus is saying that if our family keeps us from effectively serving Christ then we have made the wrong choice. We have put family in front of Him.

> "The true test of our faith is to love those who don't love us."

I have seen wonderful involvement of parents and children in the work of the church. Where that is not a clear option then there needs to be willing partners to help one another. Margaret and I have four children, so I sense something of the tension in this verse. Margaret has often not been able to be as involved in church activities as she would like because we made the decision that we would serve Christ, but not abandon our children in the process. We have taken them with us when possible, but have tried to keep a sincere and vibrant love for God and them, when we had to be apart.

Sometimes children and family are poor excuses for not being involved in kingdom work. I have often wondered what would happen if God would take from us the children we often use as an excuse for not doing what we should for His work.

At other times involvement with our children in other things keeps parents from leading their children in the truly noble things. I am an avid sports fan, but I am often appalled at the parents who get their children involved in Sunday athletics for weeks on end, thus robbing them of the valuable Godly training in the local church. Knowing that few of those children will ever make a professional team, it is a terrible spiritual injustice to the children as well as the parents. They have sacrificed the most formative and valuable years of moral and spiritual training for a few years of athletics. The trade off is not worth it. It is putting family before God. It is teaching the children the wrong value system. We need to take up our cross daily and follow Christ.

What does it mean to "take up my cross daily and follow Christ?" Is it the same for me as for you? I believe it means doing whatever is necessary to help reach my area for Christ. Simon of

Cyrene didn't expect to be called on to carry the cross of Jesus out to the place of crucifixion, but that is what was necessary that day. Not all of us will have our property confiscated, but if that is necessary then that is "our cross to carry" to follow Christ.

Churches down through the years have recognized certain things as indicators of commitment or lack of it. Several of the areas identified by the Bible and the church as necessary areas of commitment are as follows:

Godly Attitude

The Scriptural position is that our attitudes need to reflect Godliness, a concern for the lost and a love for others.

A bus was taking a group of visitors on a sight-seeing tour through New York City. At one of the stops a little lad with tattered clothes, unkept hair, and dirty hands and face stepped onto the bus. A woman asked the lady seated with her: "Where in the world is that boy's mother? Look at that dirt on him." The other woman responded, "Well, I'm sure that he has a mother, and I'm quite sure she loves him, but evidently she doesn't hate that dirt." Then she added: "I can tell you that you hate the dirt, but I don't believe you love the boy. Until loving the boy and hating the dirt can be combined, I'm afraid the boy will remain the same."

Too often we only see the "dirt" on others and fail to see their true value. We fail to truly love the person. Jesus said, "What value is it if we only love those who love us? Even totally pagan people do that" (Matthew 5:46-47). **The true test of our faith is to love those who don't love us.**

Jesus was able to combine an intense personal love for others without justifying their sin. Jesus surely does hate the sins of the world, but at the same time He loved the heart of man enough and proved it to all mankind by shedding His blood on Calvary.

Indifference to evangelism and witnessing is found too often in the church. Many never invite anyone to come to Christ or even attend services and don't intend to invite anyone. **They go on their**

merry way indifferent to a world out there that Jesus says is ripe to be harvested.

Few witness and most make no plans to witness. So much of the church never bothers to learn how to talk about Christ to a nonbeliever. We don't want the confrontation. We don't want someone to say we are a fanatic. We don't want someone to not like us. Worse yet, some have unforgiving spirits and are crippled with a spirit of faultfinding. With others there is an unwillingness to break with habits that nullify our effectiveness, habits that hinder our witness for Jesus Christ. If we fail to acknowledge our sins and make the tough decisions that need to be made we are saying, "I don't want to change. I don't want to be the kind of follower that Jesus is looking for."

Regular Attendance At Church Services

Charles Spurgeon told about a prayer meeting he attended. There was one particular Christian brother who prayed as follows: "Bless those that are home on beds of sickness and those who are home on sofas of wellness." Spurgeon goes on to say of prayer meetings, "they are regarded as tasks more than privileges by many because the people have learned to live on one meal a week."

Our prayer lists are often very long when it comes to those who are on beds of sickness, but if we are praying right, our list should be much longer for those who are home on sofas of wellness. Jesus told us not to worry about who or what can only kill the body, but be concerned about that which can destroy both body and soul in Hell. The sofa of wellness may do what Jesus warned about.

There has always been an insatiable desire on the part of committed people to be with God's people in the study of His Word. We find time to do what we want. Often that is a sad commentary on what we feel is really important. I wonder if we would have as many excuses for not being in God's house and meeting with God's people in the study of His Word if God Himself stood face to face with us when we made our excuses.

Daily Study Of The Bible And Prayer

Prayer and study brings us into communication with the head of the church. As we spend time with God we get to know His heart and will. We can share our concerns with Him. The committed church has always believed that daily time with God is necessary. The early church did it day after day after day. Failure at daily getting into the Word and prayer will cause us to fail spiritually. The two just go hand in hand. We read and pray and we survive. We forget them and we fail.

The Commitment To Ministry

People committed to Christ want to serve His church. They want to feel they are having a part in something bigger than themselves. They love Jesus and they want others to also. Such people are workers. The task doesn't have to be the most important, but if they think they are doing it for Jesus that is all that matters. In the congregations I have served, I have marvelled at the wonderful support for Kingdom work that people have given. I have seen countless hours of hard and joyful work given by people who had fallen in love with the living Lord.

On the other hand however, there are those who develop the attitude, "Let someone else do it." I have had people say, "Pastor, that's what we pay you to do." Other comments heard are "I've served my time"... "I don't want the responsibility"... or "I want to be free to go when I want to go with my camper, with my boat, to the cottage or any of the other things I want to do." Jesus said, "Pray that the Lord of the harvest would thrust out laborers into the harvest" (Matthew 9:38). Why isn't more of the harvest being brought in?

The problem is not with the harvest! Jesus said it is great—it is already a golden brown. Furthermore, none of us would accuse the Lord of the Harvest as being the problem. He certainly is fair and has done His work. The problem then has to be with the harvesters. There are simply too many members of the church sitting on the side lines watching too few members bring in the crop. There are many people involved, but too many others are only spectators. They only want to stand along side the road and watch the harvest come in. Every now and then a cheer goes up for the workers but still they do not get involved in the harvest. Is it that we have misunderstood what God said or that we don't care what God said?

The Commitment To Financial Stewardship

The average evangelical church in America gives only about 5% of its potential income to the Lord's work. In other words the church is only half obedient. If our children are only half obedient we recognize that as disobedience. We say to them, "You didn't obey. You didn't do what I said." That's the same way God must look at us. God is not necessarily asking us to sell our homes or our cars and give it all to the poor. He only asks us for a tithe and an offering. As I thought about this I don't think God is very amused at either our feeble excuses or lack of faith when we are not able to give Him at least the tenth He asks for.

Some say "Pastor, I can't afford to give." You can't afford not to give. You cannot afford to live in disobedience to the will of God. Jesus reminded us that if we are going to be His disciple it will be costly. We spend money for what we want. Such spending shows where our priorities are.

Men, I believe we are the keys. We are to be the spiritual leaders in our homes and in our churches. I believe Christ asks us to make decisions that are extremely demanding. My prayer is that God would give us more men not better methods. We have plenty of methods.

There are many wonderful promises in the Word of God, but some of them are extremely revolutionary. They call for decisions that are demanding. Costly decisions. Decisions that require time, energy and possessions and at times even our lives. With each revolutionary promise, wonderful assurances are given.

I can never figure out how people can say Christianity is for sissies. The people who say that obviously don't understand discipleship like Jesus explained it or how Jesus expected it to be lived. Sissies won't make it. They can't live it.

You may ask, "Pastor, why should I give that kind of loyalty and commitment to Jesus Christ?" Because we are committed to a real person—not a creed. We are committed to the living Lord, not some dogma of the church. After many people had deserted Jesus, He asked some of the disciples, "Will you also go away?" Peter said, "Lord, to whom would we go? You alone have the words of eternal life" (John 6:68).

10

CHAPTER

Don't Lay Low, Look Up!

*"Just as a man is destined to die once,
and after that to face judgement,
so Christ was sacrificed once
to take away the sins of many people."
(Hebrews 9:27)*

The bitter rule of Rome in the Jewish homeland was **difficult and painful for the Jews.** They were very proud and their nationalism frequently compounded the hardship. The one thing they longed for was the coming of the Messiah. For many, their hearts throbbed inside when the subject was talked about. From an early age, they had been told about the coming of the Messiah and all the things He would do for them.

The more the common people observed Jesus the more He looked like the anticipated Messiah. They thought of His miracles and His incredible teaching. Many people agreed that no man ever spoke like this before. If indeed He was the Messiah, then He would certainly throw off the yoke of Roman rule. Such was the stage as Jesus made His ascent up from the Jordan River toward Jerusalem on the Sunday before His resurrection.

The last Sunday of His earthly life, Jesus stopped first at Bethany and then proceeded to Bethphage. I had the privilege to make that same trip a few years ago, walking from those two cities to Jerusalem. I well remember recalling the passage of Scripture that described how Jesus came to the hill around Bethphage and looked over to Jerusalem.

I tried to picture Jesus as He stopped on top of the Mount of Olives, a hill top approximately three fourths of a mile east of Jerusalem. Atop Mount Olivet Jesus could clearly see the beautiful temple with its hustle and bustle. It was at this spot Jesus stopped His donkey and wept over the city. He could see the coming days of His rejection as the Christ, with the eventual humiliation and the almost total annihilation of the Jews at the hands of the Romans. He wept because the Jewish people would not receive Him as the Messiah. It was painful to have such love yet to be so ruthlessly rejected. However, this day in the life of Jesus and Jerusalem was not a day of rejection, but acceptance.

Starting at the descent from the Mount of Olives, He made His way with His entourage down the curving path, past the Garden of Gesthsemene, across the Kidron Valley and up the hill toward the walled city. The crowd continued to swell both in size and praise for the prophet from Galilee. Jesus was rebuked by the priests for letting the people praise Him but He strongly reminded them that if the people didn't the rocks would. They finally finished their ascent up the easterly side of the hill and made their way through the gate of the city with the thunderous ovation continuing.

This was it. This seemed to be the time the Romans would be cast out and defeated. No doubt many Jews were prepared to fight, crude as their instruments were.

"The promise of the return of Christ has been the hope of the Christian Church since He left for Heaven."

As Jesus wound his way through the ever busy streets, he went to the temple rather than the palace. He did little more than eject a few wicked money changers and cheats, after which He left for home. What a disappointment for the populace.

From this point on the mood of the people changed. Some of the same ones who praised him to the highest called for His crucifixion. Rather than palm branches, coats and hallelujahs, there was laughter, mocking, spit and cursing. The lowest moment in human history was now coming to a climax.

Forty days after Jesus' death and resurrection, the cruel work of the Sanhedrin having completed God's master plan of redemption, Jesus was meeting with His disciples. He talked to them about the baptism of the Holy Spirit. Again they wanted to know if this would be the time when the kingdom of God would be set up. Jesus reminded them that the timing was all in the Father's hand.

The ascension into Heaven followed shortly thereafter, again on the Mount of Olives near the spot where Jesus had wept over the city. The disciples strained to see Jesus long after he had been taken from their sight. However, an angel came with comforting words to remind them that Jesus would again return.

The promise of the return of Christ has been the hope of the Christian Church since He left for Heaven. This was a promise, one of many that Jesus had given on the same subject.

What a reception Jesus must have received as He re-entered the portals of Heaven. What great rejoicing there must have been as the angels crowded around Him! How warm the embrace he received from His heavenly Father. The best part of any trip is arriving back home and Jesus was home at last. He suffered no more cruelties, no more injustices, no more misunderstandings, no more beatings, and no more sweat, blood and tears. Gethsemane is over. Calvary is past. The tomb is empty and the Son has gone home. He has departed from the agony of earth to the adoration of Heaven. He has shifted from the bruises of earth to the blessedness of Heaven. He went from the cross to the crown. He has gone from the ghastliness of earth to the glory of Heaven. He went from the heinous treatment on earth to the haven of the Father's house.

Because of His grace, some day you and I shall be free of the earth and all of its sorrows and will be forever at home with Him. Praise the Lord!

There are individuals who criticize those who preach about the second coming suggesting that we either are in error or we put too much emphasis on it. However, it was from the lips of Jesus that this promise of great comfort was given, not only to the disciples but for Christians of every age.

His Actual Coming

The disciples were greatly saddened by the fact that Jesus was leaving them after having been with them just three short years. The Holy Spirit was part of His plan for comfort, but there were also His words in John 14:3 where he stated "And if I go and prepare a place for you, I will come back and take you to be with me that you also may be where I am." What encouragement that must have been to the disciples. They knew it wouldn't be the last they would see of Jesus.

When asked if He was the Christ, the Son of God, Jesus told the High Priest, who instigated His death, that "In the future you will see the Son of man sitting at the right hand of the Mighty One and coming on the clouds of Heaven" (Mark 14:62). Matthew's record of Jesus' discourse on the end times says, "They will see the Son of Man coming in a cloud with power and great glory" (Matthew 24:30). Hebrews 9:28 says "Christ was sacrificed once to take away the sins of many people; and He will appear a second time, not to bear sin, but to bring salvation to those who are waiting for Him."

Other verses such as Matthew 24:7; 24:36; Luke 12:40; 1 Thessalonians 5:2; Revelation 16:15; 19:11-16 not only tell of His coming but describe it in considerable detail.

However, it is Paul who in 1 Thessalonians 4:13-17, gives us the most detailed explanation of the coming of Christ for His church. He did it to overcome false teaching on the subject and as encouragement for the believers.

Paul's letter was written to Thessalonian Christians who had been waiting for the coming of the Lord since the day they first heard about Christ. They anticipated Christ would come back right away. They assumed He would have their heavenly home ready for them at any time. However, in the interim, life had gone on. They were growing older and some had even died. The church asked Paul what would happen to these people. The church was particularly concerned about when Christ would return and what would become of those who had died.

Paul is clear that the details given for the return of Christ in 1 Thessalonians 4:13-18 are from the Lord Himself. This plan was not concocted by a group of theologians, but was given by Christ either prior to His leaving earth or by a special revelation to Paul.

"We do not want you...to grieve like the rest of men, who have no hope." (verse 13)

Paul begins this portion by assuring the Thessalonians there is an answer to their questions and they did not have to wail as those without hope. Just as the Christians were to be different in their life-style, they were also to be different in response to the crises of life. Oh, make no mistake about it, there would be sorrow, tears, sadness and heartache, but it would not be that of total futility as expressed by the heathen. Paul could assure them of that.

In verse 14 Paul reiterates the heart of the gospel just as he did in 1 Corinthians 15:3. He says, "We believe that Jesus died and rose again and so we believe that God will bring with Jesus those who have fallen asleep in him." He lets it be known that the hope for the Christian is tied up in the fact of the resurrection.

1 Corinthians 15:3-4 says, "For what I received I passed on to you as of first importance: that Christ died for our sins according to the Scriptures, that he was buried, that he was raised on the third day according to the Scriptures..."

Without this truth there is no hope for anyone—all is gone. Paul ties the entire concept of the resurrection of the Christian with the resurrection of Christ.

Paul also develops the concept that when we die we go to be with the Lord. "We believe that...God will bring with Jesus those who have fallen asleep in him. (1 Thessalonians 4:14).

In 2 Corinthians 5:6-8 Paul explicitly states that the spirit of any Christian who dies goes immediately into the presence of the Lord. "Therefore we are always confident and know that as long as we are at home in the body we are away from the Lord. We live by faith, not by sight. We are confident, I say, and would prefer to be away from the body and at home with the Lord."

But that doesn't really satisfy a material thinking congregation that has difficulty separating the ideas of a physical body and the spirit. The body and spirit have always been together in life so what happens at death? What about the body? How will the body and spirit come back together? Will we recognize people? Will we have to commune with a spirit? How can we talk about going to dwell in the home God has prepared without it being something like we have known? How can a spirit dwell in the house He has prepared? We are so tied to our bodies.

This Is How It Will Happen

■ *"The Lord Himself Will Come Down From Heaven..."* *(1 Thessalonians 4:13).* There will come a time when God will command to the Son to go to earth and gather the Christians, His waiting bride. Jesus is busily preparing everything for our coming. He is working on a place for us and fitting it just for our needs.

Recently I conducted a wedding for a couple in my church. During the times I met with them prior to the wedding, the groom had talked about all the work he was doing to get the house ready for his new bride. There was work inside and out to put his place in tip top order in anticipation of moving his wife into the house.

As concerned as this new husband was for his new bride, the anticipation of Christ for His bride is even greater. He has been waiting since the time of Adam to redeem and claim His bride. The patience of the Father has been in an effort to claim as many as He can for the kingdom. But the time will come when all will be ready, the last touches put on our final dwelling place, the timing just right and the day of the Lord will have come.

Two places stand out to me in Scripture where the Godhead is intimately involved in welcoming the bride.

1. When children of God reach Heaven at death, God is there to greet them. Revelation 21:4 says, "He (God) will wipe every tear from their eyes...." As we step into the City of God with leftover concerns from our earthly pilgrimage, it is God who wipes the tears away from our eyes. He doesn't assign angels the task of welcoming the believers to their heavenly home. I like that.

I have stood at the bedside of a number of saints of God and watched them pass from this life to the next, after having fought a long and arduous battle with pain and suffering. There were tears caused by uncertainty, pain, sorrow of broken earthly relationships and unfinished projects. But what a joy to think that just on the other side of this veil of tears there is the Compassionate Creator who is there to wipe all tears from their eyes and help them come to the full realization that all the former things had passed away.

2. Christ will be intimately involved when He comes for His bride. The Scriptures indicate that angels will be involved in helping to gather in the bride but it is Jesus—the groom—who is leading the procession at His return.

Problems with self-esteem may make us question the value we have to God, whether Christ would really die for our sins or whether God really sees and knows of us. Christ cares so much

"For the believers who are alive when Jesus returns, it will be the command to drop all they are doing and proceed upward to meet Him in the air."

that He is personally coming back for us. It isn't that He cannot trust such an important role to the angels, but He doesn't want the angels to do what He desires to do.

Furthermore, He has been getting the bride ready so she will be prepared for the grand day.

Ephesians 5:25-27 says, "Husbands, love your wives, just as Christ loved the church and gave himself up for her to make her holy, cleansing her by the washing with water through the word, and to present her to himself as a radiant church, without stain or wrinkle or any other blemish, but holy and blameless."

Through the ages Christ has been in the process of refining and purifying the church. He has done it through a variety of processes, but all with the ultimate goal of presenting "to himself a radiant church."

The clouds of Heaven will be lined with people anxiously waiting for the arrival to take place. When the word is given, Jesus Himself will come from Heaven with all the deceased Christians to greet those from earth who also make up His bride. From some of my trips overseas, I know the feeling of longing for home and loved ones. I vividly remember standing in the airport in Beijing, China, after an emotionally wrenching eleven days of meeting with Chinese Christians who had been imprisoned for their faith. I looked longingly at several flights going directly to New York rather than back to Hong Kong. I thought how nice it would be just to get a New York bound flight and be home in about 15 hours. I would see my wife and children, talk to my parents, report back to my church family and be back in a land of freedom. That was appealing to me. In a similar manner, the more family and friends who have preceded us to Heaven, the greater the anticipation of Christ's return.

There are Christians on both sides—those who have already gone and those who are looking forward to Heaven, waiting to be reunited and set free from the boundaries of Satan's kingdom.

■ *"With A Loud Command" (4:16).* We are not told to whom or what this command is directed. It could be directed toward those who are currently occupying Heaven in order to get them ready to come back with Christ. It could also be a command to His angels that their work of harvesting is about to begin so they need to be ready. Furthermore, it might be likened to a command given by a leader of a group of soldiers when they are instructed to charge. There is however, one other place where Jesus gave a similar loud command.

Jesus was standing outside of the grave of His dear friend Lazarus and weeping bitterly, when He asked that the stone covering the entrance to the grave be removed. Then the Scripture says, "Jesus called in a loud voice, "Lazarus, come out!" (John 11:43). We are not told the reason for the loud shout. He could have done it with a whisper or no sound at all if He had so chosen. The loud shout seems to be Jesus' way of stirring the dead. In a same manner it may be the loud command from Jesus that calls forth the dead of millennia past to rise and be reunited with their departed spirits. For the believers who are alive when Jesus returns, it will be the command to drop all they are doing and proceed upward to meet Him in the air. I don't know whether this command will be heard by everyone everywhere or just to those with spiritual ears who currently are able to hear the voice of God and discern spiritual truths (1 Corinthians 2:9-10).

■ *"With The Voice Of The Archangel" (4:16)* The archangel is identified in Daniel 12:1 as "Michael, the great prince who protects your people" and again by name in Jude 9 as he is contending with Satan over the body of Moses.

> "Each believer will receive a new body designed by the Lord and fashioned like His resurrection body."

Daniel 12:1 further states, "At that time Michael, the great prince who protects your people, will arise... But at that time your people—everyone whose name is found written in the book—will be delivered."

It seems that Michael has the responsibility of protecting the people of God. First it was Israel, as in Daniel 12 and since then it has been the New Testament saints—the spiritual Israel. His responsibilities may include being the leader of the hosts of Heaven. This voice of the archangel will probably be directed to the angels who will be involved in bringing out the children of God.

I thrill when I see pictures of citizens lining the streets as liberating armies march into a city. I cannot help but wonder about what goes through the minds of people who have been ruled by a ruthless despot, whose armies have been cruel and inhumane, when they are set free by friendly and civilized forces. Their joy must know few restraints.

When Michael gives the command to his attending army, it will be to completely liberate the children of God from the despotic, cruel, enslaving kingdom ruled by Satan. In a moment of time the shackles of Satan's earthly rule will be lifted off, and we will escape the grip of the "prince of the power of the air." What joy and relief. What exhilaration and liberty. What peace.

■ *"With The Trumpet Call Of God" (4:16).* The passage in 1 Thessalonians 4 specifically denotes that this is the "trumpet call of God." This is God's call to the ends of the earth and the entire universe, notifying them that the great day has arrived and the marriage supper of the Lamb is about to begin.

When the president of the United States makes a public appearance his entrance is often preceded by the playing of "Hail to the Chief." In the case of monarchs it may be by a trumpet fanfare. God chooses, on the grand occasion of His Son's return, to introduce His entrance with a trumpet fanfare of all fanfares. Jesus came the first time with the quietness of a little baby, tucked back in an obscure stable during one of the busiest times of the decade. Few knew of His entrance in the manger except those to whom God chose to reveal it. However, when He comes the second time it will be with a triumphal entry fit for the King of Kings.

■ *"The Dead In Christ Will Rise First" (4:16).* My wife and I started our first full time ministry in a small church strategically situated across the road from a cemetery. Since we lived right next to the church the tombstones were in constant view. We often commented to people who stated they would never want to live this close to a cemetery, that at least we had front row seats for the next great event in God's time table of end things.

In verse 15 Paul states, "We who are still alive, who are left till the coming of the Lord, will certainly not precede those who have fallen asleep." The idea Paul wanted to emphasize was that Christians who had already died would not be left out of the resurrection. They would not be forgotten. In fact, they would go up right along with those who were still alive. They will be given a new and glorified body, as fast as an eye can twinkle.

At some point during the resurrection, the old resurrection bodies will be changed. Each believer will receive a new body designed by the Lord and fashioned like His resurrection body. At about the same time these new bodies will be reunited with their disembodied spirits that have been waiting in the presence of Jesus for this very moment. The time for the believer's glorious resurrection body has arrived.

■ Then *"We Who Are Still Alive And Are Left Will Be Caught Up With Them In The Clouds" (4:17).* These clouds are most likely indicative of the presence of the Lord, not the white fleecy clouds that encircle our earth.

During the exodus of Israel out of Egypt "The LORD went ahead of them in a pillar of cloud to guide them on their way..." (Exodus 13:21). This enabled Moses to lead such a large group of people. They had not gone far when they were attacked by the Egyptian army. It was then that the "pillar of cloud" moved behind the Israelites to provide a wall of protection. It was a wall that was not penetrable by the enemy. In the same way, the cloud will guide the rising saints and also protect the hallowed and sacred moment from the sight of the enemies of God.

■ *"To Meet The Lord In The Air" (4:17)* Somewhere between Heaven and earth Christ will meet His rising church and greet them in a similar manner as a new husband does his bride. I like to imagine there will be embraces from Christ for His bride, that we will be in awe of the splendor of the event, maybe even in wonderment that it is all taking place.

I remember working hard at my pastoral work to get all the details done so that I could take my first trip to the Holy Land. My mind had been so preoccupied with getting ready to leave that I had not given much thought to the trip itself except getting the necessary documents ready.

As I was flying somewhere across Europe it began to dawn on me that I was actually going to be walking where Jesus walked. I was going to see the places I had heard about since I was a kid. I was going to be at the place where Christ had paid the supreme sacrifice for my sins. Also I would have the opportunity to enter the tomb where He had been laid and from which He arose. It is hard to explain the feeling that came over me. I remember laying back in my plane seat and saying to myself, "Just think, I am actually going to be there. This is like a dream!" However, the thought was nothing compared to the feeling I actually felt when I was there. I couldn't help but stand in awe. I drank in every moment as I tried to visualize walking with the Savior in the Galilean hills, or sitting with Him in the Upper Room, or standing at the foot of the cross or running to the garden when the word came of His resurrection.

Will I not be filled with even more amazement as I participate in the great event of the coming of the Lord? This event that I have heard about all my life? An event that has been etched on the pages of the Bible since the time of the Old Testament? Will I be able to imagine that it is really taking place? Will you? But more importantly will you be ready for the event to take place?

■ *"So We Will Be With The Lord Forever" (4:17)* John Newton, the song writer, stated it well when he wrote, "When we've been there ten thousand years, bright shining as the sun, we've no less days to sing God's praise than when we've first begun."

The splendor of being with the Lord will be so enrapturing that not only will we be with the Lord forever, but we will *want* to be with Him forever.

My finite mind cannot imagine all that will take place. Thousands and thousands of angels plus "every creature in Heaven and on earth and under the earth and on the sea and all that is in them" will sing praises to the Lamb who is the only one worthy to receive "honor and glory and power forever and ever." (Revelation 5:11-13).

■ *"Therefore Encourage Each Other With These Words" (4:18)* My friend, do you need encouragement today? This is it. Here is the hope for every believer dead or alive. Here is the hope of the Church. Jesus is coming back to get His waiting bride.

You may be young and are looking forward to purchasing your first home or getting to cuddle your first child or test your wings in that new career. Your initial thought may be that you would like the Lord to wait awhile. But, even for you it can be an encouragement to know that the Lord is in charge of everything. As well, it should be an encouragement to keep your perspectives God centered.

To those who have lived longer, experienced much of life, and walked years with the Lord, there is great comfort in anticipating the Lord's coming.

Still others have bodies racked with disease, are imprisoned for their faith or live in Godless situations where they are attacked every day. They cry out with John the Apostle, "Come, Lord Jesus" (Revelation 22:20).

No one knows the day or the hour of Jesus' return, but we know with certainty that He is coming. Noah preached for 100 years before the rains began, but the rain did come. For millennia it was prophesied that Christ would come the first time and He did come in God's time. In God's time Christ will come the second time. The question is not if He will return, but when. He will come again as He promised.

What Should Be Our Attitude Concerning His Coming?

■ *One Of Readiness* We are to be ready for Christ's return, since He has promised to return at an hour known only to our heavenly Father (Matthew 24:36). His coming will be as unannounced as a thief burglarizing a home (Matthew 24:42-44). We will not have time to seek forgiveness from God once the command for Christ's return has been given.

■ *Involvement In The Lord's Work* Luke 19:13 says "Put this money to work until I come back." Jesus told this parable mainly because the disciples thought the kingdom would begin at once. Jesus wanted them to know there would be some time until that would happen. But the wait was not reason to quit.

Have you found your place of service in the Lord's work? Are you putting your abilities and skills to work for Him until He comes back? This is what He expects each one of us to do.

■ *Eagerly Waiting For The Return Of The Lord Jesus* "Therefore you do not lack any spiritual gift as you eagerly wait for our Lord Jesus Christ to be revealed." (1 Corinthians). Those who are ready for the Lord's return have a calmness about them. They are waiting—unhurried by necessary preparations and with great anticipation for the coming day. Titus 2:13 says it becomes a joyful expectation—"While we wait for the blessed hope and glorious appearing of our great God and Savior, Jesus Christ."

> **"Here is the hope for every believer dead or alive. Here is the hope of the Church. Jesus is coming back to get His waiting bride."**

Dr. Harry Ironside tells the story about preaching one night in Stockton, California. He was preaching about the coming of Jesus. During the final prayer he sensed someone leaving the auditorium in a rather agitated manner. While greeting the people in the foyer of the building, he noticed a woman pacing back and forth. Finally the woman engaged Dr. Ironside in conversation. She was upset that he would include in his prayer a request for the Lord Jesus to come.

She said, "I don't want Him to come. It would break in on all my plans. How dare you!"

"My dear young woman," said Dr. Ironside, "Jesus is coming whether you want it or not."

■ *Keeping The Commandments*

1 Timothy 6:14, says "To keep this commandment without spot or blame until the appearing of our Lord Jesus Christ." An evangelist of some renown was confronted about some immorality in his life. His response was that the Lord understood his physical needs and gave him a carte blanche. What he practiced in his daily life was not that which he knew God had stated in His Word. God doesn't make the exceptions many people think He does.

We are saved by the blood of Christ and only by that; however, holy living is fully expected by our Lord. To live in rebellion against the known law of God is presumption on the grace of God. If you know Him and love Him, surely your heart says "Come, Lord Jesus!"

You have often heard it said that two things can be depended on: death and taxes. Others limit that to just one: death. However, the second coming of Christ is even more sure than death because not every one will experience death. My friend, if you are discouraged or think no one sees your need or you have been forgotten, be of good courage: Christ is coming back for you. He has promised to return. Every promise of God can be depended on as sure.

11

CHAPTER

No Deposit, No Return

"Therefore, my dear brothers, stand firm.
Let nothing move you. Always give yourselves fully
to the work of the Lord, because you know that
your labor in the Lord is not in vain."
(1 Corinthians 15:58)

Wellington led his forces against the great Napoleon **in what is known as the Battle of Waterloo.** Reports of the progress of the battle were slow in coming from the battle field. In order to convey the battle's outcome, a man was placed in the tower of Winchester Cathedral to watch for a signal from a ship at sea. The message received would then be relayed across England by a similar fashion.

Finally a ship at sea was in place and flashed the message: "Wellington defeated." The fog then moved in and the man in the tower assumed the message was completed so he flashed this message for the other couriers. Soon the message of gloom was spread all over England. Some time later the fog lifted and again the ship repeated the message: "Wellington defeated." This time it added: "Wellington defeated the enemy." What a difference. The one message had spelled doom and gloom and the other was an occasion for great rejoicing. **Victory that is snatched out of apparent defeat always seems sweeter.**

Author and speaker Tony Compollo tells about a message he heard from a black pastor at a Good Friday service. The message was entitled "It's Friday, but Sunday's a comin'." Mr. Compollo tells how the pastor built on the thought of the bleak events of the Friday before Easter. The black pastor developed it on the idea that the Pharisees—proud as peacocks—were strutting around about the fact that they had persuaded the Roman government to agree to crucify Jesus. But the pastor said, "It's only Friday but Sunday's a comin'." Then those who had cheered for Him just a week earlier had turned against Christ and were pleased that this one who claimed to be the Messiah would soon be on a cross. But "it's only Friday—Sunday's a comin'." Then they hung Jesus on the cross and hurled their insults at him. But it's only Friday—Sunday's a comin'." If the message of Christ only stopped on Friday, we would indeed say, "Christ defeated." But it doesn't stop there. Sunday is here. Sunday has arrived. The message is not Christ defeated, but rather "Christ defeated the enemy."

One of the greatest needs of the human mind is to believe that there is life after death. Even those who try so hard to live a life devoid of God, often face the reality of death afraid and alone. Life after death is not a pressing issue until we face the moment of truth in our death or in someone close to us. When William Sidney Porter (whose nom de plume was O. Henry) lay dying, he said: "Turn up the lights! I don't want to go home in the dark!" Goethe, while fading away, whispered his famous last words: "Mehr Licht!" "Mehr Licht!"—More light! More light! More Light!"

Such stories of hopelessness and despair could be repeated over and over while all the time being so unnecessary. There is hope and a promise for so much more. We have the promise of a glorious resurrection. The unbelievers and the careless who face death unprepared could have it so much different if they only rested in the truth of the Scriptures.

We have the wonderful promise of the resurrection, which has been the hope of Christians down through the ages and a comfort in times of great stress and turmoil. It was written on the walls of the catacombs. It is scattered all throughout the New Testament.

The Promise Of The Resurrection

■ *The Old Testament Hope Of The Resurrection* The Old Testament saints died before the resurrection of Jesus, but yet there was hope and anticipation for life after death.

You can see that hope expressed in Moses' plea to God after the disaster with the golden calf. Moses prays, "Blot me out of the book you have written but spare the Israelites (Exodus 32:32)." Moses offered to exchange himself for his people, if that were possible. He anticipated a life after death.

Job, believed to be the earliest book of the Bible written, expresses one of the most beautiful thoughts about the resurrection as well as an expression of hope.

In the midst of the despairing words from his "friends," Job says, "I know that my Redeemer lives, and that in the end he will stand upon the earth. And after my skin has been destroyed, yet in my flesh I will see God; I myself will see him with my own eyes—I, and not another. How my heart yearns within me!" (Job 19:25-27)

Psalms 16:9-11 gives us insight into David's expectation to some day overcome the grave. Faced with the reality of death he believed God would work a miracle and redeem him from the grave. In Acts 2, Peter quotes this same passage indicating his personal belief in the resurrection as part of the eternal plan of God. Christ's resurrection was a fulfillment and confirmation of that hope.

Martha expressed an Old Testament hope, following the death of her brother Lazarus, when she said to Jesus, "I know he will rise again in the resurrection at the last day" (John 11:24). She voiced a popular doctrinal position of the Jews of her day.

■ *Jesus' Own Words* Jesus repeatedly talked about the resurrection and often of His own rising again.

"From that time on Jesus began to explain to his disciples that he must go to Jerusalem and suffer many things at the hands of the elders, chief priests and teachers of the law, and that he must be killed and on the third day be raised to life." (Matthew 16:21)

"As they were coming down the mountain, Jesus instructed them, 'Don't tell anyone what you have seen, until the Son of Man has been raised from the dead.'" (Matthew 17:9)

"When they came together in Galilee, he said to them, 'The Son of Man is going to be betrayed into the hands of men. They will kill him, and on the third day he will be raised to life.'" (Matthew 17:22-23)

"Then the Jews demanded of him, 'What miraculous sign can you show us to prove your authority to do all this?' Jesus answered them, 'Destroy this temple, and I will raise it again in three days.'" (John 2:18-22)

"Your brother will rise again... I am the resurrection and the life. He who believes in me will live even though he dies; and whoever lives and believes in me will never die." (John 11:23,25-26).

"In my Father's house are many rooms; if it were not so, I would have told you. I am going there to prepare a place for you. And if I go and prepare a place for you I will come back and take you to be with me that you also may be where I am." (John 14:2-4).

"Do not be afraid. I am the First and the Last. I am the Living One; I was dead, and behold I am alive for ever and ever!" (Revelation 1:17-18)

"Behold, I am coming soon! My reward is with me, and

> **"Do not be afraid. I am the First and the Last. I am the Living One; I was dead, and behold I am alive for ever and ever!"**
>
> (Revelation 1:17-18)

I will give to everyone according to what he has done. I am the Alpha and the Omega, the First and the Last, the Beginning and the End. Blessed are those who wash their robes, that they may have the right to the tree of life and may go through the gates into the city." (Revelation 22:12-14)

Jesus gave other claims to the resurrection in the following verses: Matthew 12:38-40; 20:18-19; 26:32; 27:63 Mark 8:31-9:1; 9:10; 10:32-34; 14:28,58; Luke 9:22-27; John 2:19-22; 12:34.

Jesus assured the thief on the cross that he would be ushered into God's presence that very afternoon of his death (Luke 23:43).

Luke records for us in Acts 1 that before Jesus was taken up into heaven, He appeared to His close followers and "gave many convincing proofs that He was alive. He appeared to them over a period of forty days."

I have read various accounts of the death and resurrection of Jesus. Of all the events that surround Jesus' appearance to His disciples following His resurrection, I think I would have enjoyed most being one of the two individuals on the road to Emmaus (Luke 24:13-35). They had the privilege of Jesus explaining all the passages of the Old Testament that talk of Himself. I would love to hear Jesus teach through Genesis to Malachi. I would thrill to have Him show me all the places He is referred to and how all these events had their fulfillment in Him.

In spite of all the evidence of the literal and physical resurrection of Jesus, some still deny it. The denial of His resurrection is a denial of the work of Jesus.

Paul writing in 1 Corinthians 15 talks a great deal about the resurrection. At the start of the chapter, he particularly targets those who deny the resurrection.

Starting in verse 15 he says that **if you deny the reality of the Resurrection:**

■ *"Not even Christ has been raised from the dead."* If we deny the possibility of our resurrection, then we also must deny the reality of Christ's resurrection. You can't have one without the other.

■ *"Our preaching is useless."* There is no reason for anyone to go door-to-door to invite people to Christ, or stand in a pulpit and preach or go from place to place sharing the good news of the gospel. For if Christ has not been raised from the dead and if you will not be resurrected, then our preaching is useless.

■ *"Our faith is useless."* Why believe? The Apostle Paul goes on to say that those who deny the resurrection of believers are false witnesses about God. Those who preach the resurrection of Jesus, but deny that Christians will be raised from the dead, are lying about Jesus.

■ *"We are still in our sins."* Furthermore, if Jesus didn't rise from the dead people are lost even though they believed in Him. Such people are to be pitied.

Christianity stands or falls with the truth of the resurrection.

If someone could disprove the resurrection then Christianity would crumble. Either Jesus can be trusted with what He said about the resurrection or He can't be trusted at all.

Paul wrote that if there is no hope of resurrection, then Jesus was never resurrected. And if Jesus was never resurrected, that means Jesus was a liar and a lunatic and not Lord.

I have tremendous confidence in the reality of His victory over the grave. The advancement of other religions, especially the influx of eastern religions, reminds me that there is no other religion on the face of the earth that makes claim to a risen Savior. None. No religion can claim that their founder/savior is alive.

Our Resurrection Body Will Be
Far Superior To Our Earthly Body

People generally wonder, especially in this appearance conscious age, what our resurrection body will be like? What will it look like? Can we feel? Can we taste? Will we be able to eat? You may have questions of your own about it.

Pastors often discuss the subject of the resurrection body during a funeral service, while surrounded by beautiful flowers. Paul gives us insight into that question in 1 Corinthians 15:37 when he says, "When you sow, you do not plant the body that will be, but just a seed, perhaps of wheat or of something else."

I remember meditating on this verse one day, when it dawned on me that the seeds that were planted to produce beautiful flowers were nothing like the beautiful flowers. Paul says the seed that is sown doesn't compare in looks in any way with the flower that is produced by that seed. The seeds have to die and decay and then are raised to a new life. So it is with us. The new body of ours will be unspeakably beautiful in comparison to the body that is planted: just like the flowers are many times more beautiful than the bulbs or seeds from which they grow.

Whenever I stand by the bed of one who has just died, and I look on that body, I am reminded of Paul's words in 1 Corinthians 15:42 where he says, "The body... is sown perishable... in dishonor... in weakness and a natural body." Along with family members, I choke back the tears in what appears to be a hopeless and dismal situation. There is nothing more hopeless than a dead corpse. The body that once laughed and was filled with vitality and vigor now lies lifeless and cold.

Not long after death the process of decay begins. The Apostle Paul says about the body of the believer, "It is sown perishable, but is raised imperishable, it is sown in dishonor, but it is raised in glory, it is sown in weakness, but it is raised in power, it is sown just a natural body, but it is raised a spiritual body" (1 Corinthians 15:42-

44). Sometimes when I view a lifeless body lying in a hospital room or in the funeral home, I think for a moment "Christ defeated!" and then realize that the complete truth is "Christ defeated the enemy!" Praise should raise from our lips every time we see a flower and are reminded of this valuable truth.

You may have friends restricted to a bed who are unable to move. If they are believers, you can remind them that some day they will move as freely as the angels in heaven. You may have a loved one whose body is emaciated by the terminal effects of cancer. They will be given a body that knows nothing of disease. Old age will be a thing of the past. There will be no senior citizen housing with the depressing scenes of shriveled-up human forms. That will all be gone, for we who are in Christ will all receive a new and glorified body.

Our Resurrection Body Will Be For All Eternity

The Apostle Paul received word that there were those at the church in Thessalonica who were concerned about those who had already died. It was commonly believed in that day that Jesus would come back while they were all alive. Then Christians died. They wondered what happened to these people? Where were they? Would they be forgotten? Would they be a part of this resurrection message?

So Paul wrote these words of comfort starting in 1 Thessalonians 4:13, "Now friends, about those questions you have about people who have died in the Lord. Let me share a few thoughts. This very same Jesus will come back with a shout, with the voice of the archangel, and the trumpet of God, and the dead in Christ shall be raised first" (Hossler paraphrase). They would not be forgotten. In fact they would come forth first.

Those who died in the time of the Apostle Paul have been dead almost 2,000 years. They have not yet received their glorified body. But their spirit has gone to be with the Lord. When Christ returns,

> "Christianity stands or falls with the truth of the resurrection. If someone could disprove the resurrection then Christianity would crumble. Either Jesus can be trusted with what He said about the resurrection or He can't be trusted at all."

they will be changed and given their glorified body. For those in poor health, time goes so slowly. They feel they have been ill so long that they wonder when it will ever end.

Our brief life time will seem even shorter in eternity. It is so fleeting even now. When Margaret and I go calling on some of our shut-ins, most of them older people, one of the things we hear in most every home is, "My, how times flies. How quickly these years have passed." Take heart dear sufferer, you soon shall be passed from this life to the next.

Paul further shares that the change will be instantaneous:

"Listen, I tell you a mystery: we will not all sleep, but we will all be changed—in a flash, in the twinkling of an eye, at the last trumpet. For the trumpet will sound, the dead will be raised imperishable, and we will be changed." (1 Corinthians 15:51-52)

You have heard it said that we are only a heartbeat away from eternity. You understand the meaning of that, but may I also add that we are only a heartbeat away from a glorified body.

This may be the generation that sees the coming of the Lord. Not everyone alive today may die. But those alive when Jesus comes shall be changed. How quickly? "In a flash, in a twinkling of an eye" (1 Corinthians 15:52).

The Promise Of The Resurrection
Is A Call To Godly Living

Many people of Paul's day did not believe in the resurrection and
had no hope for the future. Paul describes such a situation in 1
Corinthians 15:32 when he says "There are those who are saying let
us eat and drink, for tomorrow we may die." Why not live as
selfishly and foolishly as we know how for we are the only ones we
have to please? We are like some animal that comes and lives for a
few years and we go into the grave and that's it.

Paul said "How foolish." Don't be mislead. Quit your sinning.
Because Jesus died, was buried, but rose again on the third day, you
too are a participant in resurrection.

You will be given a glorified body, instantaneously, therefore,
this is how your are to live. Notice the keys the Apostle Paul gives
us in 1 Corinthians 15:58:

■ *"Stand Firm—Be Unmovable."* This is a defensive posture.
Don't be quickly pushed aside. Don't let any person or thing shake
your faith in the work of Christ. Don't give in to materialism, or be
persuaded by an unbeliever. Don't even shrink back from
persecution. Stand firm in the Lord.

■ *"Always give yourself fully to the work of the Lord."* Don't
give up your worship attendance or your Bible study. Don't quit
living a Godly life in an ungodly world. Consider your priorities.

Sometimes we see people struggle with "giving themselves fully
to the work of the Lord" when they are asked to get involved
somewhere in the Lord's work. They don't seem to have the time.
They don't want to be involved. They want to do other things.
They want to live their life for themselves. Paul reminds us to stand
firm in the Lord and remain involved in His work.

■ *"For you know that your labor is not in vain in the Lord."*
Some say there is no resurrection. Others live like there is no
resurrection. But we know there is hope beyond the grave. There is
a coming judgement when we will stand before the King of the
Universe to be rewarded for the things done while in this body

> "Listen, I tell you a mystery: we will not all sleep, but we will all be changed—in a flash, in the twinkling of an eye, at the last trumpet. For the trumpet will sound, the dead will be raised imperishable, and we will be changed."
>
> (1 Corinthians 15:51-52)

whether for good or for evil. Therefore, he says, your labor is not in vain. Jesus said that even a cup of cold water given in His name will not go without reward. Just think how all the labors of love that you give in His service will be remembered. Where are you storing up the greatest dividends? Jesus said, Don't store up treasures on earth where they can be stolen, decay or rust away. But store up treasures in heaven where none of those things can affect them (Matthew 6:19-21). Your labor in the Lord is not in vain (1 Corinthians 15:58). It will be rewarded.

Friend, the only hope you have for the resurrection is to commit your life to Christ and seek His forgiveness.

What if today, the trumpet would sound, you would hear the voice of the archangel and Jesus would return? Does that thought strike fear in your heart or does your heart leap for joy? Have you made preparations and are you ready to meet Him?

The Washington Post quoted President George Bush after he returned from a visit to Russia:

"An amazing thing happened at the funeral of Soviet leader Brezhnev. Things were run with military precision; a coldness and hollowness pervaded the ceremony: marching soldiers, steel helmets, Marxist rhetoric, but no prayer, no comforting hymns, no mention of God. I happened to be in just the right spot to see Mrs. Brezhnev. She walked up, took one last look at her husband, and there—in the cold, gray center of that totalitarian state—she traced the sign of the cross over her husband's chest. I was stunned. In that simple act, God had broken through the core of the Communist system." Mrs. Brezhnev's simple act as she traced the cross, whether in secret belief or tremulous hope, showed that the message of a crucified, risen Savior cannot be excluded by an iron curtain or an atheistic regime.

Jesus Christ traced the sign of the cross over our cold gray world nearly 2,000 years ago. Since that time, countless individuals and governments have tried to bury Him, but He always proves Himself alive just as He did that first Easter morning.

12

CHAPTER

Pay Day In Paradise

"Store up for yourselves treasures in heaven
where moth and rust will not destroy and
thieves do not break through and steal."
(Matthew 6:19)

The Word of God makes room for only two groups of
people in the world today. It describes them as those that
are saved and those that are lost. Or put another way,
"those who have the Son and those who do not have the
Son" (1 John 5:12). Just those two groups. The Bible does not
leave any room for fence straddlers. It does not leave any room for
those who say they want to be a little bit of both.

Jesus and the world are not going in the same direction.
They are going in opposite directions. We must be aligned with one

or the other. Jesus said we could not be part of His kingdom and part of the world as well (Matthew 6:24).

The promises of God are not limited just to the righteous. There are also promises for those who are not righteous, for those who have not accepted Christ as their Savior. The rewards are divided between these two groups of people. There are promises for the righteous and promises for the unrighteous.

Promises For The Righteous

There are many promises for those who suffer because of their faith in Christ. We in America know little about that aspect of the Christian faith. However, all you have to do is read Hebrews 11 or church history and you soon discover that thousands of people have suffered because of their Christian faith.

Jesus says in Matthew 5:12, "Rejoice and be glad when you suffer because great is your reward in heaven." In 2 Timothy 2:12 Paul says, "If we endure we will also reign with Him." In the book of Hebrews 10:34 it says, "You sympathized with those in prison and joyfully accepted the confiscation of your property," Why? Why would they joyfully accept it when people would come and take things away from them because of their faith in Christ? The reason they did so was because they knew that they "had better and lasting possessions." There is a promise for those that suffer because of their faith.

A Heavenly Home

There is the promise of a heavenly home. This is what Jesus was talking about in John 14 when He said, "I am going away to prepare a place for you and when it is ready I will come and get you so you can be with me where I am."

We have some concept and glimpse of an eternal home in the Old Testament. When he was praying for the children of Israel who had sinned in the wilderness, Moses asked God to blot his name out of the book, but please spare these people. God let Moses know

> "The Book of Life contains a registry of all those who put their faith in Christ. These are the ones who will have a home in Heaven."

that this was one area that was off limits to Moses (Exodus 32:32-34). David in the Psalms said, "I have this confidence that the Holy One will not see decay nor will He abandon my soul to the grave" (Psalms 16:8-11; Acts 2:25-28). David anticipated far more than merely the grave. He looked forward to a rich and rewarding afterlife. He expected all believers to dwell in a heavenly home.

There are some things we notice about this heavenly home that are an encouragement to us.

■ *Safe Deposit For Our Treasures* "Store up for yourselves treasures in heaven where moth and rust will not destroy and thieves do not break through and steal" (Matthew 6:19). The things that we do for the kingdom's sake are deposited in that home He has prepared for us.

■ *Registry* There is a registry of all those who have declared themselves to be on God's side and who have accepted Him as Lord and Savior. The disciples, upon returning from their mission trip said, Master, we touched these people and they were healed and even evil spirits that had controlled some of these people for so long were subject to us. It was just great. Jesus, you ought to have been there to see it. Jesus said, Men, don't get so excited that the demons are subject to you, but rather get excited that your name is written in heaven" (Luke 10:20). The Book of Life contains a registry of all those who put their faith in Christ. These are the ones who will have a home in Heaven.

In Revelation 20:15 we read, "If anyone's name was not found written in the book of life, he was thrown into the lake of fire."

The wicked are brought up for the great white throne judgment and a search is made for their name in the book of life. If their name is not found, they are cast into the lake of fire.

■ *God's Mansion* It is a home that has been built by God's hand. In John 14:2 Jesus said, "In my Father's house are many rooms; if it were not so, I would have told you. I am going there to prepare a place for you." In other words, he told them he was going away to build it. 2 Corinthians 5:1 says, "Now we know that if the earthly tent we live in is destroyed, we have a building from God, an eternal house in heaven, not built by human hands." Colossians 1:5 says pretty much the same thing: "The faith and love that spring from the hope that is stored up for you in heaven and that you have already heard about in the word of truth, the gospel." Jesus said He was God and He was going away to build us a place.

■ *All Are Welcome* There will be no language, cultural, or color barriers in heaven. There will be room for all the redeemed. In Revelation 7:9, John writes: "After this I looked and there before me was a great multitude that no one could count—from every nation, tribe, people and language, standing before the throne and in front of the Lamb. They were wearing white robes and were holding palm branches in their hands." None of God's children will be turned away from their eternal home.

■ *A Place Of Great Beauty* I encourage you to read Revelation 21, verses 11 through 21. I want to describe this place for you but it is almost beyond description. Its walls are transparent gold. Its gates are of a single pearl. Every foundation is of a different kind and color of stone. The street of the city is pure gold, but appears like transparent glass. It is a place that none of us in our finite minds can possibly imagine.

■ *No Ills* We won't know any of the ills we know here. There will be no sorrow, pain, crying, night or death. Jesus said that in heaven everything is made new. Heaven is made up of a whole new creation while these other things are made up of the past. All the things that have troubled us down through the years will be gone and forever passed away.

■ *Crowns* The believer will receive spiritual crowns. In 1 Corinthians 9:25, we are reminded that there is a crown that will last forever. Also we receive a crown of righteousness, a crown of life and a crown of glory. In Revelation 4:10 we find that those who have gathered around the throne are taking their crowns and laying them all before the Lamb, as if to say: Oh Jesus, you are the only reason we are here. We have been rewarded with these crowns for the things we have done while in this life, but they are nothing compared with what You have done for us. You have helped us to get here. You have been the only means for our salvation.

Charles E. Fuller once announced that he would be speaking the following Sunday on "Heaven." During the week a beautiful letter was received from an old man who was very ill. The following is part of his letter:

"Next Sunday you are to talk about Heaven. I am interested in that land, because I have held a clear title to a bit of property there for over 55 years. I did not buy it. It was given to me without money and without price. But the Donor purchased it for me at tremendous sacrifice. I am not holding it for speculation since the title is not transferable. It is not a vacant lot.

For more than half a century I have been sending materials out of which the greatest Architect and Builder of the universe has been building a home for me which will never need to be remodelled nor repaired because it will suit me perfectly, individually, and will never grow old.

Termites can never undermine its foundations for they rest on the Rock of Ages. Fire cannot destroy it. Floods cannot wash it away. No locks nor bolts will ever be placed upon its doors, for no vicious person can ever enter that land where my dwelling stands, now almost completed and almost ready for me to enter in and abide in peace eternally, without fear of being ejected.

There is a valley of deep shadow between the place where I live in California and that to which I shall journey in a very short time. I cannot reach my home without passing through this dark valley of shadows. But I am not afraid because the best Friend I ever had went through the same valley long, long ago and drove away all its gloom. He has stuck by me through thick and thin, since we first became acquainted fifty-five years ago, and I hold His promise in printed form, never to forsake me or leave me alone. He will be with me as I walk through the valley of shadows, and I shall not lose my way when He is with me.

I hope to hear your sermon on heaven next Sunday from my home in Los Angeles, California, but I have no assurance that I shall be able to do so. My ticket to heaven has no date marked for the journey—no return coupon—and no permit for baggage. Yes, I am all ready to go and I may not be here while you are talking next Sunday evening, but I shall meet you there some day."

There are tremendous promises for the future life for those who are followers of the Lamb.

Promises For The Unrighteous

There are also promises given for those who are not followers of the Lamb and they are just as true and accurate and sure as for those that are followers.

When we were young we would often play hide and seek. Mom and dad would stay around church to talk and fellowship and we kids would go outside and play. Usually there was some kid that found an ideal hiding place and could never be found. Periodically we would have to say, "All, all in free." Everyone could come in and not be tagged "it." There are many who believe that sometime God is going to say, "All, all in free." They claim it makes no difference what you have done, what you have believed, how you have behaved or how you have acted. All are in free. But they do not get that promise from the Scriptures. The Scriptures are clear concerning the promises of the rewards for those who are not followers of Jesus Christ. I would not be true to my calling or my Lord if I did not warn you and plead with you concerning this particular truth.

During World War II there was a troop ship carrying American soldiers on its way to battle. A number of soldiers had gathered around the chaplain and someone had asked, "Sir, do you believe in hell?" To which the chaplain replied, "No, I do not." To which the man responded, "Then if there is no hell, we think you ought to resign because we don't need you and if there is a hell we don't want you to lead us astray."

There is coming a day of final separation when the lost and the saved will be separated eternally. Jesus, telling the story in Matthew 13:24-30, says there was a farmer who planted a crop of wheat. Sometime later the enemy went out and sowed all kinds of weeds in that soil. After a while both the wheat and weeds began to grow. The servants came in and told the owner of the crop that someone had sowed weeds in this beautiful crop of wheat. When they asked whether or not they should take the weeds out, the owner said to leave it all there to grow up together. At the time of harvest, he told them, we will separate out the wheat and put it in the barns. We will then bundle the weeds and throw them into the fire.

Later, as Jesus gathered in a home with some of his disciples, several of them asked Jesus what he had meant by the story about the wheat and weeds being separated. Jesus told them that the field is the world, the good seed stands for the sons of the kingdom and the bad seed stands for sons of the evil one. The enemy that sowed the bad seed is the devil himself, the harvest is the end of the age and the harvesters are the angels. When the harvesting process begins all those who do evil will be gathered as were the weeds. They will be bound and thrown into the fire where there will be the weeping and gnashing of teeth.

Jesus told another story about the separation of the sheep and goats. The goats were gathered on His left hand and went off to destruction while the sheep were gathered to the right—the sheep being followers of the Lamb (Matthew 25:31-34). In Luke 17 Jesus says there will be two in the bed—the one will be taken and the other one left. There will be eternal separation between the two.

Luke 16 records the story of the rich man and Lazarus. The rich man seemingly had everything he could desire. He had all the wealth and luxuries of a prosperous man of his day. He was the envy of his fellow man: the epitome of success. But, he had little care for his fellowman and even less care for God.

Then there was another man whose name was Lazarus. Lazarus was so poor that he had nothing of this world's goods. He had no livelihood, no medical care and no strength, but he did have a great love for God.

The rich man would have gotten along fine if life would have stayed as it was. He had everything going for him. He had all his heart could desire. But the Scripture records these two little sentences, "The beggar died and the angels carried him to Abraham's side. The rich man also died..." (Luke 16:22). The rich man would have been fine if he wouldn't have died. But he did! It is a fact that everyone must someday come to that same dilemma. No longer was the rich man being judged by the court of public opinion: the court that had been saying, "Yeh, we like what you are doing and we want to follow you." Now he was being judged by God himself. The standards of God and public opinion are entirely different since God looks on the heart while man only looks at the outward appearance.

There are several things to note from this passage.

Starting in verse 23 the scene changes from heaven to hell. "And in hell, where he was in torment, he looked up and saw Abraham far away, with Lazarus by his side. So he called to him, 'Father Abraham, have pity on me and send Lazarus to dip the tip of his finger in water and cool my tongue, because I am in agony in this fire.'"

From this Scripture passage, we conclude the following:

■ *Death brought immediate judgment.* There was no second chance here. There was no way this rich man thought he was going to work his way out of hell. There was no way God was going to pull a fast one and by some means, through the back door, let him come in free. I am afraid many are living under the false assumption that somehow, someway they will be bailed out of a Christless eternity. Friends, according to the Bible, that will not happen. Hebrews 9:27 says, "...as man is destined to die once, and after that to face judgment...."

Nowhere does the rich man consider he will receive a second chance. Nowhere do we even hear him asking God to somehow show him some more grace or to help him to get out. We find him praying to send someone to his brothers and tell them not to come to this place. But he does not believe that he's going to get out.

■ *Hell is a place of torment.* The rich man asked Lazarus to dip his finger in a glass of water and drop it on his tongue because of the torment caused by the flames. There are those who try to attack this particular part of judgment. Friend, if you will read your Bible you will find out how often the Scriptures talk about the punishment and torment that comes with the eternal judgment of the lost. Read for yourself from the words of Jesus and others. Isaiah 33:14; 66:24; Matthew 3:12; 13:42; 18:8; 25:41; Revelation 14:10. In Revelation 20:15 we read, "If anyone's name was not found written in the book of life, he was thrown into the lake of fire." Revelation 21:8 says, "But the cowardly, the unbelieving, the vile, the murderers, the sexually immoral, those who practice magic arts, the idolaters and all liars—their place will be in the fiery lake of burning sulfur. This is the second death."

I wish I didn't have to tell you one thing about these terrible promises, but Jesus said, "These things are trustworthy and true" (Revelation 22:6). They are promises. They are statements of fact just as much as Psalms 23 says, "The Lord is my Shepherd, I shall not want." They are just as true. But I notice something else about this place.

■ *We will remember.* One thing that will be extremely well-honed in hell is one's memory. Luke 16:25 says, "But Abraham replied, 'Son, remember....'" Memories will be sharp. I think the rich man must have thought of all the opportunities he had ever had: the times when he had spurned the love of God, when he had rejected those who pleaded with him to have some mercy on the beggar and when he laughed at an invitation to turn to the Lord. I wonder if he said, "Get out of here. I don't want to hear it. I don't have time for it now." Now he remembered.

Anyone who sits through a gospel message, but does not respond to the gospel will remember the opportunities they missed. Memory is a powerful tool and in hell it will be keen.

■ *Separation* There is a great chasm between the righteous and the wicked. Luke 16:26 reminds us, "And besides all this, between us and you a great chasm has been fixed, so that those who want to go from here to you cannot, nor can anyone cross over from there to us." It is a chasm that God has created between the two worlds. On the one side is a Christless eternity where one will be forever away from the presence of the Lord. It was designed primarily for the devil and his angels. Everything they stand for will be there.

Yes, heaven and hell are both very real places. You cannot believe in the one without believing in the other. You cannot say on the one hand that you only want to believe in heaven, but not in hell. They are both frequently talked about in the Bible. There are many, many promises that are given to both the righteous and the lost concerning their future rewards.

My prayer is that you will not miss heaven. There is absolutely no need for anyone who has ever heard the gospel to lose out on their eternal home with Christ. The Bible promises that if you will ask Him to come in and cleanse you from your sins He will do it (John 1:9). You may say, "But pastor I'm not that bad. I think I'm OK." There were those who Jesus dealt with who felt the same way. They thought they could do it their own way. They felt that somehow, by their own good works, they could climb over the gate and make it.

I remember reading a story about a man who had a dream that he was climbing the ladder to heaven. Every good deed he did took him one step higher. He was almost to the top when the ladder collapsed and he fell crashing to the ground. He then remembered the verses in the gospel of John where Jesus said that if one tries to get into heaven by any other method than through Christ he is a thief and a robber. Jesus is the only door (John 10:1). There is no other way. We can do good and we can have good intentions, but we can't get to heaven without Christ.

There were others that Jesus told about who missed out simply because they were careless. In the story of the ten virgins (Matthew 25:1-13), five of the women brought extra oil and the other five brought only what was in their lamps. The bridegroom didn't come as quickly as they anticipated, but late one night the shout rang out that the time had finally arrived. The ones who had brought the extra oil poured it into their lamps and the others realized they had no more oil and their lamps were going out. The latter wanted the first group to share with them, but there wasn't enough. The latter five had to go out and buy from the people who sold oil. When they got back to the house, the bridegroom had already arrived, the door was shut and there was no admittance (Matthew 25:11-12).

Individuals, like the latter five virgins, who try to get into heaven on the faith of others, will not make it. Saving faith cannot be shared with someone else. Each individual must use such faith to obtain their personal eternal salvation from the only one who can grant it, Jesus Christ.

Still others pretended to be followers of Jesus. They used His name in attempting to heal and cast out demons. They came to Jesus and showed Him what wonderful things they had done in His name. Jesus told them he was sorry, that he did not know them, that they were not one of his. He called them pretenders, counterfeits. (Matthew 7:22-23)

Some so called followers thought disobedience would not disqualify them—that somehow God would overlook their sins. Revelation 21:8 says, "But the cowardly, the unbelieving, the vile, the murderers, the sexually immoral, those who practice magic arts, the idolaters and all liars—their place will be in the fiery lake of burning sulfur."

I am afraid that some who have listened to the gospel have not come clean. Even in the church there are people involved in immorality, drinking and drunkenness, sinful attitudes, unforgiving spirits, and lying. Maybe by your own admission you would say that your life is not much different from someone making no claim to being a Christian. May I remind you that God asks believers to live a life of holiness. He has called us to be peculiar people—a different people. The way of the world and God's way go in opposite directions. They are completely different. There will be no "all in free". Now is the day of grace. Today when we hear His voice we need to say yes.

In verse seventeen of the last chapter of Revelation it says, "The Spirit and the bride say, "Come!" And let him who hears say, "Come!" Whoever is thirsty, let him come; and whoever wishes, let him take the free gift of the water of life." All the time you hear Jesus saying, "Come! Come! Come!" He doesn't want a single person to miss out on the glories of heaven.

I believe there will be no way for those who miss heaven and are sent to an eternal hell to ever shake their fist at God and say, "You never warned me!" or "You never told me!" God will begin to point out all the road blocks He had placed in their way and the opportunities that were theirs to turn from their wickedness to follow Christ. This is particularly true of the road block of the cross.

How is your relationship with the Lord? If He were to come today, do you have the promise of eternal life? We can have. 1 John 5:13 says, "I write these things to you... so that you may know that you have eternal life." Why not receive Him right now?

References

Chapter 2

p.11   James Montogemery Boice, **The Gospel of John (An Expositional Commentary, Vol. 1** (Grand Rapids, Zondervan Publish Co. 1975), p. 236.

p. 14   Paul Lee Tan, **Encyclopedia of 7,700 Illustrations:Signs of the Times** (Rockville, Maryland: Assurance Publishers, 1979), p. 1130

p.15   Boice, p. 226-228

p.18   Boice, p. 278

p.20   Boice, p. 276.

Chapter 3

p.25   Tan, p. 492.

p.28   Tan, p. 507.

p.28   Paul E. Freed, **Let The Earth Hear.** Thomas Nelson Publishers, Nashville, ©1980, p. 191-192.

p.29   F. C. Jennings, **Studies in Isaiah** (Neptune, NJ, Loizeaux Brothers, 1935), p. 417.

p.30   Tan, p. 1569.

Chapter 4

p.32   Walter B. Knight, **Knight's Treasury of Illustrations** (Grand Rapids: Erdmans Publishing Co., 1963), p. 265.

p.39   Tan, p. 1525.

p.41   Tan, p. 480-481.

Chapter 5

p.54   **Autoillustrator**. Illustration #12113, P.O. Box 5056, Greeley, CO 80632

Chapter 6

p.58   Tan, p. 1527.

p.64   Tan, p. 886.

Chapter 7

p.68 Tan, p. 1153.

p.73 Tan, p. 1152.

Chapter 8

p.96 R. T. Kendall, **Tithing: A Call To Serious, Biblical Giving** (Grand Rapids, MI. Lamplighter Books, 1982), p. 41.

p.97 Kendall, p. 19-20.

p.97 Kendall, p. 20.

p.98 Kendall, p. 92.

p.98 Kendall, p. 103.

Chapter 9

p.100 Robert Coleman, **Master Plan of Evangelism** (Los Angeles, Rusthoi Publications, 1963), p. 112.

p.104 Coleman, p. 76.

p.106 J. Walter Hall, Jr., Christian Clippings, February, 1990 (Wesley Chapel, FL 33543), p. 20.

Chapter 10

p.125 Tan, p. 1638.

Chapter 11

p.128 Tan, p. 1509.

p.128 Knight, p. 102.

p.138 Pulpit Helps, AMG Volume 15, Number 7 (Chattoonga, TN, 1990), p. 19.

Chapter 12

p.144 Tan, p. 545-546.